Colorado

Mountain Passes

View looking north from Red Mountain Pass.

Colorado

Mountain Passes

The State's Most Accessible High-Country Roadways

TEXT AND PHOTOGRAPHY BY

Rick Spitzer

WESTCLIFFE PUBLISHERS

www.bigearthpublishing.com

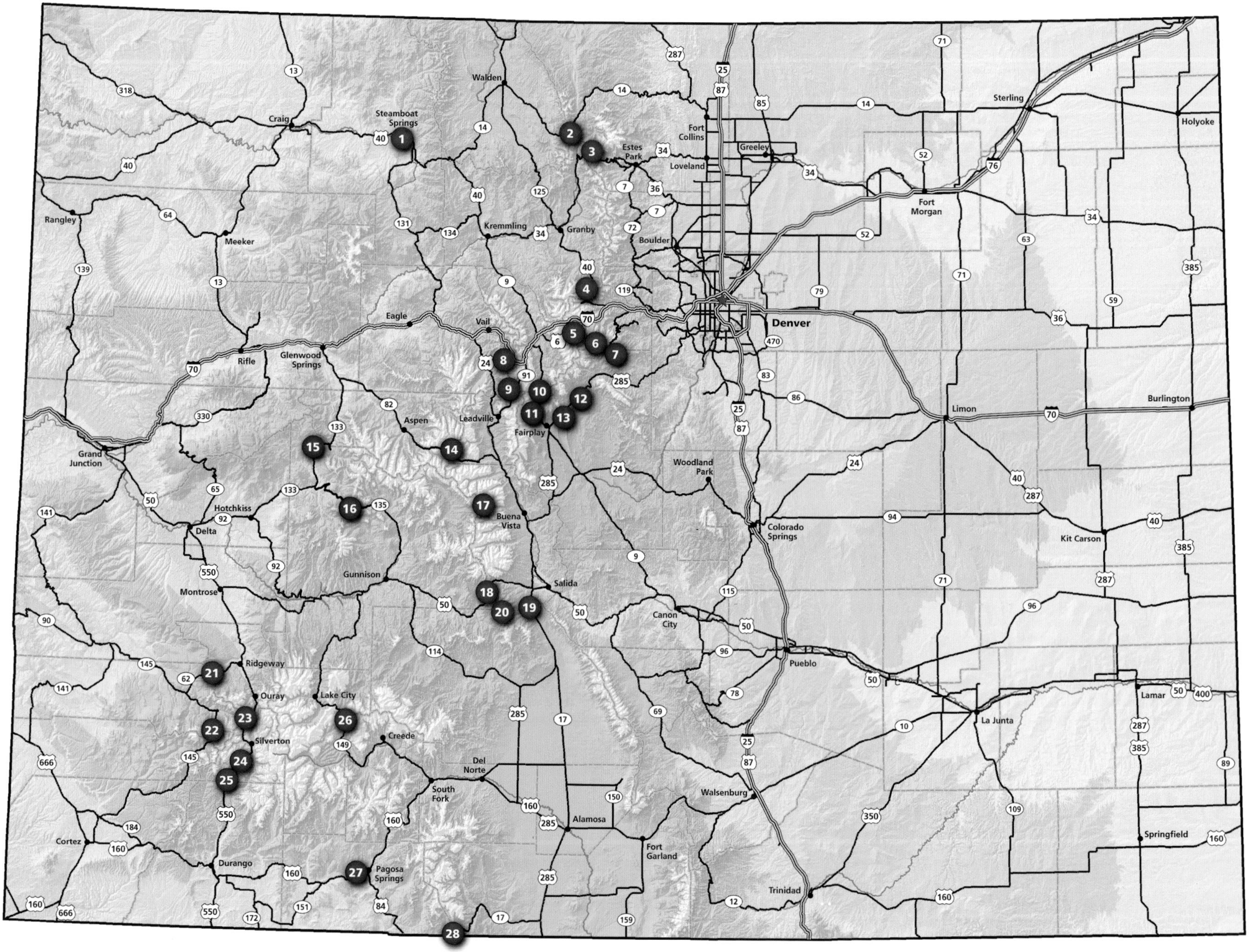

Walden
Steamboat Springs
Craig
Fort Collins
Estes Park
Loveland
Greeley
Sterling
Holyoke
Fort Morgan
Rangley
Meeker
Kremmling
Granby
Boulder
Denver
Eagle
Vail
Rifle
Glenwood Springs
Aspen
Leadville
Fairplay
Limon
Burlington
Grand Junction
Woodland Park
Hotchkiss
Delta
Buena Vista
Colorado Springs
Kit Carson
Gunnison
Salida
Montrose
Canon City
Pueblo
Ridgeway
Ouray
Lake City
Silverton
Creede
La Junta
Lamar
Del Norte
South Fork
Walsenburg
Alamosa
Cortez
Durango
Pagosa Springs
Fort Garland
Trinidad
Springfield

Contents

Longs Peak and surrounding mountains, as seen from Trail Ridge Road in Rocky Mountain National Park.

Introduction

I grew up in Colorado, and when I was a kid my father loved to get the family together in the '40 Ford and hit the road. My mom put together picnics that had every kind of olive, pickle, potato chip, salad, lunchmeat, cheese, and cookie you could imagine. She would make my dad drive for miles looking for that perfect lunch spot. We traveled across the plains, into the mountains, and over many of Colorado's mountain passes. The scenery out the window always impressed me. I anticipated some new adventure around every bend in the road. Our trips covered almost every state highway in Colorado at a time when many of those roads were still dirt. We saw a lot and learned a lot about our state! What a time in my life! Looking back, I would not trade those days for anything.

Today, many millions of drivers and their passengers cross the same mountain passes and enjoy the same spectacular scenery that my family and I enjoyed. As I hiked and studied these areas as an adult, I discovered many important bits of history tied to them. The easiest route from one point to another over a mountain range often takes advantage of a pass, and many of Colorado's mountain passes have been used by humans for centuries—some even longer. The routes over them helped shape Colorado into what it is today.

This book provides a unique understanding of Colorado's passes, and will hopefully serve as a valuable resource for those traveling them. But more than that, it is a photo-driven reflection on these special places. Many of the photos presented in this book are distinctive because they are true panoramas of the scenes. The panoramas take in more than the eye can see, with some offering a full 360-degree view. Each pass includes at least one of these special images, along with a black and white version of the panorama indicating the cardinal directions as well as the names and elevations of nearby peaks. I also included photographs of interesting sites at each pass location as well as the surrounding areas. Occasionally, historical photos from the late 1800s are included to show how the area looked then. Whenever possible, I have also tried to match the historical scene with a photo of the same scene today.

Colorado Mountain Passes: The State's Most Accessible High-Country Roadways offers the reader a matchless scenic view of the state and a unique historic perspective. *Enjoy*!

What is a Pass?

For the purpose of this book, I've chosen to define a pass as a low point in a mountain range that separates two watersheds. Theoretically, a bucket of water dumped on the top of a pass would split, with some water flowing down one side of the pass into one river drainage and the rest flowing down the other side into a different drainage. Other terms used to designate a pass are gap, ridge, and divide. Several well-known mountain highways cross passes on the Continental Divide, which separates the continent's Mississippi River Basin (which drains into the Atlantic Ocean) from the Colorado River Basin (which drains into the Pacific Ocean).

Since passes are low points in the Rocky Mountain Range, they provided the preferred routes for travel across the mountains for Native Americans, mountain men, wagon trains, railroads, and eventually automobiles. Many of the routes over Colorado's mountain passes have been around for centuries. Some reflect changes made to accommodate trains and early automobiles that could not handle the steep grades of the original footpaths or wagon roads.

Passes are often the highpoints of the highways that cross them, but not always. Trail Ridge Road—the highest continuously paved highway in the United States—has a high point of 12,183 feet in Rocky Mountain National Park, though it crosses Milner Pass at 10,758 feet.

Rifle Sight Notch on the old railroad grade of Rollins Pass, north of Berthoud Pass.

The Ten Highest Colorado Highways

1. CO 5, Mount Evans—14,160 feet*
2. US 34, Trail Ridge Road—12,183 feet*
3. CO 82, Independence Pass—12,095 feet
4. US 6, Loveland Pass—11,992 feet
5. CO 9, Hoosier Pass—11,541 feet
6. CO 149, Slumgullion Pass—11,361 feet
7. CO 91, Fremont Pass—11,318 feet
8. US 40, Berthoud Pass—11,315 feet
9. US 50, Monarch Pass—11,312 feet
10. I-70, Eisenhower Tunnel West Portal—11,158 feet.*

* Highway whose highpoint is not located on a pass

Though most of the passes in Colorado are scenic and reach high elevations, a driver may not even be aware that they are crossing a pass except for signage telling them so. Not all high-elevation roads cross passes. In fact, two of Colorado's highest roadways do not. The Mount Evans and Pikes Peak roadways terminate at the summits of the respective peaks. I considered this book incomplete without information on the Mount Evans road, which is rich in both history and scenery. I have included it as the only "non-pass" highway in this compilation.

Other Resources

A number of historians and cartographers have compiled data on the passes of Colorado. James Grafton Rogers recorded many Colorado geographical features and names. Rogers served as the first president

For each pass in this book, I have included the following information:

PASS NAME: The name of the pass as it appears on signs at the location or maps of the area.

ORIGIN OF NAME: The source for the name that is applied to the pass.

ELEVATION: The elevation of the pass above sea level as it is listed on the Official Map to Colorado.

NEARBY CITIES: The nearest towns or cities on opposite sides of the pass. Cities are listed south to north or west to east.

POINTS OF INTEREST: Geologic features, national forests, historic landmarks, and other notable features.

COUNTY: The county in which the pass is located.

HIGHWAY: The federal (US), state (CO), or county highway that crosses the pass. Even-numbered highways move traffic west/east and odd numbered highways move traffic south/north.

MILEPOST: Most highways have mile marker signs on the side of the road measuring mileage from the border of the country, state, or county. Highways oriented west to east begin the measurement starting in the west. Highways oriented south to north begin the measurement starting in the south.

GPS COORDINATES: The GPS (Global Positioning System) coordinates listed indicate the north and west coordinate of the location of the pass. The GPS can assist a person using a GPS unit to locate any point on the earth to within a few feet. GPS units translate data, received from satellites orbiting the earth, into degrees, minutes, and seconds.

TOPO MAP: The topographic map that the pass can be found on.

DIRECTIONS: Directions to the pass will begin from the two closest towns on either side of it.

126°

This symbol illustrates how many degrees of view the picture encompasses. At the center is the person looking at the scene; the band of gray represents what he is seeing. If the band makes a full circle around the person, that indicates a 360° panorama.

of the Colorado Mountain Club and as a long-standing president of the Colorado State Historical Society, so he knew our state very well. Ralph Brown, an Instructor of Geography at the University of Colorado in 1925, also compiled a list of passes published in *Colorado Magazine* in 1929. Marshall Sprague's important historical reference on passes, *The Great Gates: The Story of the Rocky Mountain Passes*, was published in 1964.

Ed and Gloria Helmuth compiled an extensive list of passes and their histories in *The Passes of Colorado: An Encyclopedia of Watershed Divides* (1994). Their book is the most extensive study of Colorado's passes, and includes virtually all named passes found on detailed maps, whether trails or roads traverse them. Many of the 460 trails and roads listed no longer exist. Ninety-two of them cross the Continental Divide.

The Official Map to Colorado prepared by the Colorado Department of Transportation contains many interesting pieces of information about Colorado roadways. It lists thirty-eight passes on state and federal highways. With county and forest service roads included, the total number of listed passes on Colorado roads approaches 200.

Colorado Highway Passes

Pass	Elevation (Ft)	Highway
Berthoud	11,315	US 40
Boreas *+	11,482	Forest 33 and 10
Cameron	10,276	CO 14
Coal Bank	10,640	US 550
Cochetopa *	10,032	County NN14
Cottonwood	12,126	County 306
Cucharas	9,941	CO 12
Cumbres	10,022	CO 17
Dallas Divide	8,970	CO 62
Douglas	8,268	CO 139
Fremont	11,318	CO 91
Guanella *	11,669	County 381
Gore	9,527	CO 134
Hoosier	11,541	CO 9
Independence +	12,095	CO 82
Kebler +	9,980	County 12
Kenosha	10,001	US 285
La Manga	10,230	CO 17
Lizard Head	10,222	CO 145
Loveland	11,992	US 6
Marshall *+	10,846	Forest 243.2 and 200
McClure	8,755	CO 133
Milner +	10,758	US 34
Molas Divide	10,910	US 550
Monarch	11,312	US 50
North La Veta	9,413	US 160
Muddy	8,772	US 40
North Pass	10,149	CO 114
Poncha	9,010	US 285
Rabbit Ears	9,426	US 40
Red Hill	9,993	US 285
Red Mountain	11,018	US 550
Slumgullion	11,361	CO 149
Spring Creek	10,901	CO 149
Squaw	9,807	CO 103
Tennessee	10,424	US 24
Trout Creek	9,346	US 24/285 Ute 9,165 US 24
Vail	10,666	I-70
Wilkerson	9,507	US 24
Willow Creek	9,621	CO 125
Wolf Creek	10,850	US 160

* Passable dirt road + Closed in winter
Passes on highways over the Continental Divide in **Bold**

Mountain Ecology

Aspens

Some people joke that summer occurs on the peaks of the Colorado Rockies on July 17th between three and four o'clock in the afternoon. For every 100 feet of elevation gained, spring comes one day later and fall comes one day earlier. As a general rule, the temperature drops 5.5º F for every 1,000 feet of elevation gained in a dry, stable air mass. That means that when it's 80º F in Denver, it may be 50º F on top of Vail Pass. For people into trivia, this is called the "adiabatic lapse rate." Summer snowstorms frequently occur in Colorado's high country. The short seasons and cold temperatures dictate the kind of flora and fauna found in the Rocky Mountains.

Each pass illustrated in this book lies in one of three major life zones found in Colorado's mountains: the montane, subalpine, and alpine. Unique features dictated by elevation—including soil, moisture, drainage, and exposure—impact the characteristics of each life zone. Because these zones overlap each other, you usually cannot define a clean boundary between them. These vague boundaries, called "ecotones," are often great places to spot wildlife.

Very specific plants and animals live in each life zone. After evolving for hundreds of years with no interference, the species of vegetation growing in a specific area stabilizes to create what ecologists call "climax vegetation." Because animals depend upon plants for food and shelter, the type of animals in a life zone vary according to that zone's vegetation. Other factors, such as temperature and exposure, also determine which animals live in which life zone.

Top: Elephants head. Second row: Monkshood, Blue columbine. Third row: Bistort, Spotted coral-root orchid, Fleabane, Avalanche lily.

Left to right: Purple pincushion, Red columbine, Blue flax

Kinnikinnick

Kinnikinnick is a low-growing plant with shiny leaves and red, waxy berries. Its scientific name is *Arctostaphylos uva-ursi*. *Arcto* and *ursi* are words for "bear" and *staphlos* and *uva* are words for "berry" or "grape." The scientific name means "bear berry berry bear," and its common name is bearberry.

The Montane Zone

The area from about 6,000–9,000 feet is called the "montane zone." The average annual precipitation in this zone is 20–30 inches. Aspen, located to the west of Independence Pass (pg. 134), lies in the montane zone.

The climax vegetation in this zone includes ponderosa pine, Douglas fir, lodgepole pine, and aspen. Asters, Indian paintbrush, chiming bells, flax, monkshood, and the Colorado state flower, the columbine, are also typical to the montane zone. Shrubs in this zone include mountain ash, arnica, thimbleberry, serviceberry, wild raspberry, and kinnikinnick.

Mountainsides, open valleys, and the areas near water sources all support different climax vegetation. Vegetation on drier, south-facing slopes is often made up of mountain mahogany and sagebrush. Douglas fir and lodgepole pine dominate cool, moist, north-facing slopes.

Douglas fir can also survive in dryer environments. They grow fast and, for this reason, fill an important niche in the forest industry of North America. They also supply many of our Christmas trees.

Between the mountain ranges in some Colorado locations lie broad, flat areas, called parks, which are devoid of trees. Parks often capture less rainfall and snowfall, making them drier than the surrounding hillsides. This creates an excellent habitat for ponderosa pines, as seen in South Park near Kenosha Pass (pg. 124). Ponderosas' large size and wide spacing make them easy to identify from the highway, and the very distinctive vanilla odor in their bark makes them easy to identify up close.

The state tree, the Colorado blue spruce, thrives in the moist areas around streams and creeks. This tree's square, sharp needles, coated with a white powder, give it a distinctive bluish cast, making it easy to identify. Alder, narrowleaf cottonwood, and willows are also found along streams and riparian corridors.

Brush and grass grow in the open areas under these widely dispersed trees. Because of this, livestock grazing is common in the montane. However, this vegetation tends to dry out quickly and is highly flammable, making fire a fairly common event in these areas. Surface fires burn the forest understory every 20–30 years, and fire is an important component of this ecosystem. Douglas fir and ponderosa pines can survive forest fires that do not get too hot. Their thick, corky bark protects the living inner tissue.

A lone ponderosa pine stands before a montane forest of lodgepole pine and Douglas fir.

Lodgepole Pine

These trees are rarely mistaken for other pine trees. They love the sun and grow in thick stands. Really dense concentrations of lodgepole are called "dog hair" stands. As you wander through them you feel like a flea on the back of a dog.

Pollen cones on a lodgepole pine.

Lodgepole pines require bright sunlight. Because of that, combined with the fact that they grow in such thick stands, growth occurs only in the crown of the tree. The needles and branches on the lower parts of the tree die and drop off, producing a tall, thin trunk—perfect for teepee poles.

When blown free by a gust of wind, the pollen of these trees creates incredible yellow clouds that can darken the sky. This fine yellow dust covers the ground, picnic tables, and the surfaces of puddles.

Lodgepole forests rely on fire to survive. When fires come through, they wipe out older trees while allowing the pinecones—which are sealed closed by a resin that must be melted by fire—to open and release their seeds. Without fire, the stands reach an unhealthy old age, where they are susceptible to insect invasions and disease. In the absence of fire, lodgepole stands in the montane zone will eventually be replaced by spruce–fir forests.

A grove of sun-loving aspen.

Moraines

Many montane areas of Colorado contain noticeable ridges of debris called moraines. During the last ice age, 15,000 years ago, the glaciers acted as conveyor belts, depositing debris as they moved. They formed these moraines along their sides (lateral moraines) and ends (terminal moraines). Some of the terminal moraines dammed rivers when the glaciers retreated, forming ancient lakes. Over time, the lakes filled with silt and plant debris, which often resulted in large, flat wetlands with deep, peaty soils. Meandering streams pass through these wetlands, which support a wide variety of plants and animals.

Aspen, a member of the poplar family, is considered a pioneer species because it frequently spreads into areas that have been disturbed by fire or logging. Aspens are sun-loving trees and, like lodgepole, often grow in dense groves. They have tall trunks with green leaves only on the crowns of the trees. Because aspen cannot grow in their own shade, after their lifespan of 75 to 100 years they are often replaced by Engelmann spruce and subalpine fir.

The Subalpine Zone

The elevation from 9,000 feet to around 11,500 feet comprises the subalpine zone. The subalpine zone experiences a short growing season with extreme temperature changes. Snow covers the ground from late September to April. The subalpine receives about 30–40 inches of precipitation per year. From the summit of Independence Pass (pg. 134), you can look down on the subalpine zone.

Spruce-fir forests grow at all altitudes and in almost all the environments of the subalpine, making it the most common forest

Parry primrose blooms along a creek in the subalpine zone.

Alpine tundra along Trail Ridge Road in Rocky Mountain National Park. Longs Peak is visible in the distance.

in the zone. Limber pine and bristlecone pine can be found in the upper limits of the zone near treeline. Aspen grow in its lower parts, often in areas recently destroyed by fire. Lodgepole pine grow in the warmer, drier areas of this zone. Common flowers in the zone's wet areas include Parry's primrose and marsh marigold; drier areas nurture Colorado columbine, wild rose, fireweed, lupines, and calypso orchids.

A number of Colorado's parks fall into the elevation range of the subalpine zone. Grass is the predominant vegetation in many of these parks, including North Park near Cameron Pass (pg. 46), South Park near Boreas Pass (pg. 108) and Kenosha Pass (pg. 124), and the San Luis Valley near Poncha Pass (pg. 172). Spruce-fir forests surround these flat, grassy areas.

Fires are not as common in the subalpine because of its cooler temperatures and higher moisture. Additionally, the understory does not accumulate much highly flammable vegetation. Only every few hundred years are there fires severe enough to burn through the crowns of the trees.

The Alpine Zone

The zone extending from 11,500 feet to the summit of the peaks also goes by the name "alpine tundra,"—tundra being a Russian word meaning "land of no trees." The summit of Independence Pass (pg. 134) lies at the lower end of this zone, and 11 miles of Trail Ridge Road (pg. 51) cross the tundra.

The alpine zone experiences extreme temperature fluctuations that vary from 70° F during the day to below freezing at night, even during the month of July. In winter, snow blows across this wind-swept area, creating bare spots in some places and deep snow pack

A yearling mountain goat relaxing on the tundra.

in others. The growing season at this elevation lasts only a few weeks. Precipitation, including snowmelt, can reach 40 inches per year.

Tundra in Colorado resembles the tundra of the far North, but because the mountain slopes here are well-drained, it does not contain a permafrost, or permanently frozen layer of ground. Many of the tundra plants growing in Colorado resemble plants that grow in the Arctic. Plants growing in the alpine zone require special adaptations for survival. Here are some of the ways these plants survive:

- They grow quickly to make it through the short growing season.
- They stay close to the ground, which has a more constant temperature than the air, to escape frequent freezing and thawing—short plants also avoid damage due to the high winds.
- Some have waxy or hairy leaves, which help to prevent moisture loss.
- Some have clear hairs that absorb and store heat from the sun.
- Many contain anthocyanin, a chemical that absorbs heat.
- Some have large, thick roots to store food each season.
- Some bloom only every few years.
- Often, plants grow together in clumps in order to retain moisture.

Typical alpine zone plants include grasses, mosses, lichens, and willows, as well as snowberry and bog birch. A number of wildflowers, including alpine primrose, alpine forget-me-not, phlox, alpine sunflower, purple fringe, king's crown, sky pilot, arctic gentian, alpine lily, alpine sandwort, and golden draba add color to the tundra during this zone's short summer growing season.

Some protected, moist areas of the tundra hold clumps of small willows. They hug the ground, over time providing protection for other willows growing near them to form larger and larger clumps. Many birds and animals use the willows for protection during severe weather.

Tundra ecosystems are very delicate and care must be taken to protect them. Plants and animals specific to the tundra generally do not migrate—there are some species that only exist in a single tundra region in the whole world! Because of its short growing season, damaged tundra takes many years to recover. Visitors at overlooks or around heavily used trailheads should stay on the trails to avoid contributing to this damage. One or two tramplings by hikers crossing the tundra probably causes little damage. After all, deer, elk, and bighorn sheep travel across the tundra daily and pay no respect to staying on the trails. Damage occurs when multiple tramplings a day destroy the vegetation. Please stay on trails in heavily visited areas. Enthusiasts who like to hike on the tundra should do so only in areas that are not heavily used. Use the alpine tundra lightly!

Treeline

Trees do not grow in alpine regions because they cannot survive in the harsh environment. The average elevation of treeline in Colorado is 11,500 feet, and the average daily temperature there is below 47° F. Treeline occurs at lower elevations on north facing slopes and as you travel north across the state and the country.

Ferocious wind and snow often distort the trees that grow at treeline. They are stripped of vegetation on their exposed sides, resulting in some very oddly shaped trees with polished bark and wood. These forests are called "krummholz," which is a German word for twisted wood. They are also known as "goblin forests." Subalpine fir, Engelmann spruce, limber pine, and bristle cone pines often form these krummholz. Trail Ridge Road (pg. 51) and Mount Evans (pg. 82) reveal some of the best examples of krummholz in Colorado.

Left: Banner trees such as these are the result of strong winds that strip the vegetation off the upwind side of the tree. Below: A limber pine in a goblin forest at treeline.

Limber pine krummholz.

Mountain Wildlife

The high country of Colorado supports a wide variety of wildlife. These animals must survive a broad range of conditions, including temperatures that can range from between 80° F in the summer to -30° F in the winter. The unique vegetation of each life zone helps us predict what animals will live there. This does not mean that animals typical to one zone cannot be found in another. For example, deer, elk, and bighorn sheep roam all three high-country life zones, depending on the time of year and the weather conditions.

Animals typical to the montane zone include:

- deer
- elk
- bighorn sheep
- black bears
- mountain lions
- chipmunks
- golden-mantled ground squirrels

Animals typical to the subalpine zone include:

- coyotes
- elk
- marmots
- pine marten
- black bears
- chipmunks
- mice
- voles
- golden-mantled ground squirrels

Animals typical to the alpine zone include:

- ptarmigan
- pikas
- marmots
- mountain goats
- bighorn sheep
- pocket gophers

Here is a closer look at some of the animals you might find in the high country.

Mammals

Rocky Mountain Bighorn Sheep *Ovis canadensis*

The Rocky Mountain bighorn sheep is the Colorado state mammal. It uses all three high-country life zones. Males grow the massive,

curving horns that are the most distinctive characteristic of the bighorn. Females also have horns, but they do not develop to the same size.

Bighorns prefer open areas and find sanctuary on cliffs. They remain active during daylight hours and can often be found along roadways, where they congregate to enjoy the salt deposited by the

highway department to clear snow. Bands of sheep generally segregate themselves according to sex during most of the year; the males and females intermingle during the November and December mating season.

During mating season, the males engage in amazing head-butting battles. First, they face each other from about 30 feet apart. Then, by some unknown cue, they rise up on their hind legs and hurl themselves at each other, crashing head to head, sometimes in mid-air. They can collide at speeds of up to 20 mph! The smash of their horns creates an impressive sound, causing the observer to wonder how they survive the impact.

> Horns are similar to fingernails in many ways. Their bone interior is covered by an exterior sheath, which, like your fingernails, is grown by specialized follicles. The composition of that sheath is very similar to that of your fingernails, too. Horns are never shed and, for most animals, they grow continually, forming annual rings that can be used to determine the animal's age—the only exception to this rule is the American pronghorn, described later in this chapter.

Elk *Cervus elaphus*

The name "elk" causes confusion internationally. In Europe, the name elk belongs to the animal we call moose. American elk are also called wapiti, a name given to them by the American Indians that means "light-colored deer."

Elk graze mostly on grasses and forbs, and sometimes, during the early morning and late evening hours, you can see them grazing

in open meadows and on the alpine tundra. Elk feed most actively at night and tend to take sanctuary among trees during the day.

Elk are the second largest member of the deer family and grow to an impressive size—bull elk often weigh over 750 pounds. The large, distinctive antlers of bulls can weigh 25 pounds and spread over 4 feet. These antlers grow to their huge size in less than 6 months. Even though antlers consist of the same material as bone, they are shed every winter or spring. Only bull elk carry antlers, which they use to assert their dominance in mating rituals during the fall.

Elk mating, or "rutting," season occurs around mid-September. During this time, elk congregate in meadows in herds sometimes numbering in the hundreds. Bulls compete for the attention of females, called cows, and try to defend those in their harem. The bulls challenge each other with loud bugles that can be heard for miles. The sound mixes a strange combination of guttural noises and whistling.

Males often spar with each other by joining antlers and engaging in incredible shoving matches. One bull will eventually overcome his rival due to his superior strength and stamina. Sometimes, while these matches distract the larger, older bulls, a young bull sneaks in and mates with one of the cows.

Mule Deer *Odocoileus hemionus*

A mule deer's dark brown or slightly gray coat allows it to blend easily into its environment. They feed mostly on woody shrubs and tend to travel in small bands of three or four. The bucks weigh up to 250 pounds and, like elk, shed their antlers in late winter.

As their antlers begin to develop in the spring, a furry skin, called velvet, covers them. In the fall when the rut begins, the deer rub their antlers against trees and bushes to remove the velvet. It is believed that when the blood supply to the antlers diminishes in the fall, the skin on the antlers begins to itch. The rubbing may provide relief from the itching rather than be an intentional act to scrape the velvet off.

Mule deer are one of only two species of deer that inhabit Colorado. The other is the whitetail deer, which populates the plains and some of the foothills of the Rockies. The mule deer prefer the higher elevations of the mountains, but their range sometimes overlaps with that of the whitetail deer.

If you can remember just a few key characteristics, you will be able to distinguish a mule deer from a whitetail deer. Mule deer have very large, mule-like ears. Their tails are narrow and black tipped; whitetail deer have a broad tail with a white underside. The antlers of the species also differ. Mule deer antlers branch into Ys, while whitetail antlers have a single beam with numerous tines.

Mountain Goat *Oreamnos americanus*

Mountain goats may not be indigenous to Colorado. Early accounts describe mountain goat sightings in the 1880s, but the observer may have confused them with bighorn sheep, as often happens today. In 1947, the Colorado Division of Wildlife (DOW) transplanted 14 mountain goats from Montana into the Collegiate Range. Later, other mountain goats arrived through arrangements with British Columbia. The DOW originally introduced them to provide trophy-hunting opportunities. The Colorado Wildlife

Commission proclaimed the Rocky Mountain goat a native species in 1993.

The shaggy, white wool coat that is the mountain goat's most distinctive trait can also be its most deceiving one. Some people mistake them for sheep! Mountain goats are certainly not sheep and, interestingly, they are not really goats either. Though they are in the same subfamily, *Caprainae*, as both goats and sheep, they are the sole North American species in their genus, *Oreamnos.*

This unique animal is the largest mammal living in its high-altitude habitat. Males, or billies, grow up to 5 feet long and weigh up to 250 pounds. They look much bigger because of their thick coat.

This coat tends to become somewhat yellow and mangy in the summer. In late summer and early fall mountain goats shed their coat; large mats of it can be observed hanging loose from their sides. By late fall they once again show a beautiful coat of solid white.

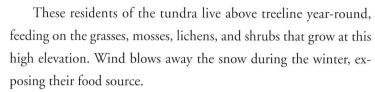

These residents of the tundra live above treeline year-round, feeding on the grasses, mosses, lichens, and shrubs that grow at this high elevation. Wind blows away the snow during the winter, exposing their food source.

Mountain goats can often be observed scrambling around on rocks and steep cliffs with no apparent concern for heights. They often walk out to the edge of a cliff or onto large rocks to survey their territory as if they were enjoying the scenery. Because they have no natural predators on the tundra, they remain active during the daytime. Mount Evans (pg. 82) provides one of the most accessible areas in the state to encounter mountain goats.

Moose *Alces alces*

The name moose is an Algonquian word meaning "twig eater." These large animals—the largest members of the deer family—are not considered indigenous to Colorado. When European explorers first came into the Rocky Mountains they reported few sightings of moose. However, many moose have been transplanted into the state during the last twenty years. They are now reproducing well and becoming fairly common in many parts of the state. Moose tend to favor the montane valleys where they feed on willows and other moisture-loving plants.

One way to identify moose is by their very distinctive palmate antlers. The areas between the antler tines fill with bone. Moose have a very deep brown or black coat that helps distinguish them from the elk, which are brown with a darker shoulder and a tan rump patch. Moose are solitary animals, but can sometimes be sighted in groups of two or three. They weigh more than 1,000 pounds, stand 5 to 6 feet at the shoulder, and will fiercely defend themselves or their young.

Pronghorn *Antilocapra Americana*

Colorado is home to the fastest animal in North America and the second-fastest land mammal on earth. The American pronghorn can reach speeds of 70 mph—only the African cheetah is faster. Not

only are pronghorn fast, they can maintain speeds of 60 mph for up to 4 miles and keep cruising at 30 mph for another 5 miles. Pronghorn often race along with cars out of the sheer joy of running. An oversized windpipe, huge lungs, and a large heart help them accomplish these incredible speeds.

The pronghorn also has exceptionally large, protruding eyes, which can detect the movements of predators up to 4 miles away. The pronghorn's name comes from their uniquely shaped, pronged horns. Pronghorn are the only animal in the world to shed their horns annually.

The scientific family name *antilocapra* means "antelope goat," but pronghorn are neither an antelope nor a goat; they are the sole surviving member of a family that originated in North America sometime before the last ice age. These animals can withstand desert heat as well as winter cold. At one time, their numbers in North America may have exceeded that of the bison.

To see pronghorns, visit the large parks of Colorado. North Park west of Cameron Pass (pg. 46) and South Park southwest of Denver are great choices.

Red Fox *Vulpes vulpes*

Two species of fox live in Colorado: the red fox, which has a red coat and a white tip on its tail, and the gray fox, which has a gray coat and a black tip on its tail. The red fox is more common.

The thickness of its fur makes a red fox appear much larger than it really is. A red fox will eat just about anything that does not eat it first. Rabbits, rodents, birds, reptiles, amphibians, insects, eggs, fruit, and carrion comprise its diet.

During the winter, fox live in dens that they dig themselves or claim from previous rodent residents. They often form monogamous relationships and may hunt in pairs. They breed in winter and may have as many as ten pups.

Long-Tailed Weasel *Mustela frenata*

This weasel sports a stylish fur coat throughout the year. In the summer the coat is a rich brown with sulfur yellow highlights. In the winter, however, that would attract a lot of attention on white snow, so it molts to pure white. The weasel with this white coat is often called an ermine.

The tip of this weasel's tail is always black. Some believe the black tip protects it from predatory birds during wintertime. A bird dropping out of the sky may grab for the distinctive black spot on the snow, allowing the weasel to escape.

Their long, slender bodies allow weasels to enter the dens of chipmunks and ground squirrels, some of their favorite prey. When they are above the ground, weasels often move with a very distinctive arched back. They are curious and will often sit up to watch or even follow a hiker. Weasels live in rocky, brush-covered areas from the montane to the alpine tundra.

The author with a black bear that was captured, tranquilized, and fit with a radio collar in Rocky Mountain National Park.

Black Bear *Ursus americanus*

The American black bear is the only species of bear currently living in Colorado. Although there is some evidence that grizzly bears roamed Colorado mountains in the past, most reported sightings of the grizzly today are suspect.

The coat of the black bear can be black, brown, blonde, or cinnamon colored. They can run close to 30 mph, climb trees, and swim well. Black bears living in the Colorado Rockies are small in size, usually weighing between 150 and 250 pounds. Because of their reputation and thick fur, people often mistake them for being about twice as large as they really are.

A bear's diet consists mostly of vegetation. Black bears will rarely kill a large animal for food. Insects, grubs, berries, bulbs, fruit, fish, and small animals make up the majority of their diet.

> **Do bears hibernate?**
> Bears go dormant during the winter, but, contrary to rumor, it is not the true hibernation of squirrels and other smaller mammals. During true hibernation, an animal's body temperature drops to just a few degrees above freezing, their respiration and heart rate are barely discernible, and they are very difficult to rouse. Though bears do not eat, drink, or eliminate wastes when they are dormant, their body temperature, respiration, and heart rate do not drop dramatically, and they remain somewhat active.

Bears go dormant during the winter, but, contrary to their reputation, they don't actually hibernate. They consume astounding quantities of food before they retreat to their winter dens and again when they come out in the spring—about 20,000 calories per day, or ten times what a human eats. When hungry bears forage for food in mountain communities, it can lead to trouble.

Mountain Lion *Felis concolor*
A full-grown mountain lion measures more than 6 feet from head to tail. Their tail accounts for one third of their total length. Their coats are typically tawny colored, but they can range from gray to reddish brown.

The mountain lion's range is one of the largest of any mammal in the Americas, extending from parts of Canada all the way across North America and into South America. Their local names include puma, cougar, painter, catamount, panther, and screamer.

Mountain lions exemplify the ultimate stereotype of a predator with their stealth, strength, and grace. Their speed and ability to leap 20 feet in the air make them legendary. People rarely see them in the wild, however, because of their stealth and cunning. Mule deer provide the vast majority of their prey, and studies have shown that lions need one deer per week for survival. They also prey on bighorn sheep and elk.

Yellow-Bellied Marmot *Marmota flaviventris*
The largest kind of squirrel in Colorado is the marmot. They are most often found in rock piles above treeline. Whistle pig, groundhog, woodchuck, and rockchuck are just a few of their nicknames. Their large size, brown to yellowish-brown coat, yellowish belly fur, and distinctive whistle make them easy to identify.

Marmots are often found sprawled out on a rock soaking up the sun. They tend to be more active in the afternoons, when they forage for plants. Because they hibernate during winter, marmots put on a lot of weight in the fall.

Chipmunk *Tamias*

Chipmunks are found throughout the Rockies, from the foothills all the way to the alpine tundra. They are one of the most familiar animals to Colorado campers because of their propensity to beg for food at overlooks and in campgrounds. There are several species of chipmunk that inhabit Colorado, and all have similar appearances.

Seeds comprise the primary diet of chipmunks. They often gather the seeds, pack them into their cheeks, and take them to their burrows to be stored. Chipmunks spend the winter in their burrows in a state of torpor. Because they may move around to feed on stored food or, if it is especially warm, even leave their burrows, chipmunks are not said to be hibernating.

Richardson's Ground Squirrel *Spermophilus richardsonii*

This ground squirrel inhabits almost all areas of the state from border to border, but rarely ventures above treeline. Because of their habit of standing upright, they are sometimes called a picket-pin, a name derived from a stake used to tie up a horse. They prefer sunny slopes and dig extensive burrows that they tend to stay close to.

As with most squirrels, they subsist on plants, put on weight in the fall, and are deep hibernators in the winter. They have short ears and a brownish-gray coat with no distinctive markings.

Golden-Mantled Ground Squirrel *Spermophilus lateralis*

Chipmunks and golden-mantled ground squirrels look somewhat similar, but are quite different upon close inspection. Chipmunks are smaller and have stripes on their heads. Golden-mantled ground squirrels have chipmunk-like stripes on their bodies, but no stripes on their heads, a fuller body, and a shorter, bushier tale.

Ground squirrels prefer rocky areas along the edges of forests. They feed on stems, leaves, seeds, berries, and fungi. They will also eat insects and carrion. Like chipmunks, they enter their burrow in the winter, roll into a ball, and enter a state of torpor.

Pika *Ochotona princeps*

Pikas look a lot like camouflaged guinea pigs. This little animal is actually a cousin of the rabbit, though its body form and round ears do not resemble a rabbit's at all. One of the pika's many nicknames is rock rabbit. This is because they live in talus slopes and boulder fields near and above treeline. Because they stay active throughout

the day, pikas are easy to spot. They are even easier to hear. Most people who have hiked in the high country have heard this animal's loud, high-pitched chirp.

A pika's diet consists mostly of herbs, but they eat other plants as well. They act like alpine farmers, gathering vegetation into "hay piles" (sometimes larger than a bushel in size), which they then store under rocks.

Even though pikas live in a very cold climate, they do not hibernate. During the winter they live near or in the hay piles, eating themselves out of house and home as spring approaches. Interestingly, they produce two kinds of feces; one is hard and considered waste, but the other is soft and considered food—it is re-ingested to pass through the digestive tract a second time.

Nuttall's Cottontail *Sylvilagus nuttallii*

Nuttall's cottontail is the smallest of three species of rabbits found

in the mountainous areas of the state. Jackrabbits and snowshoe hares, its cousins, share the same range. You can identify the cottontail by its reddish brown fur and black-tipped ears. They inhabit forest edges, where they are sheltered and hidden by brush. They are mostly active at night, but can be seen occasionally during the day.

Nuttall's cottontails feed year round. During the warm months they eat grasses and forbs, and during the cold season they subsist on dry grass, bark, and twigs. These rabbits give birth to four to six blind, hairless young that require a great deal of care before they can leave the nest.

Birds

Steller's Jay *Cyanocitta stelleri*

Of the three jays common to the Rockies, the Steller's jay is the most distinctive. Its dark blue body, black head, and a tuft of white feathers in front of its eyes makes it easy to identify, although it is often mistakenly called a blue jay.

Steller's jays live in the forest, where they fly noisily between perches and the ground, picking up seeds and nuts. As with most jays, the Steller's jay learns quickly that campsites are a good source of food.

Georg Steller, an eighteenth century German naturalist, documented this bird while traveling with Vitrius Bering when the latter discovered the Bering Strait. The Steller's jay now carries his name.

Clark's Nutcracker *Nucifraga columbiana*

This jay, named after the famous American explorer William Clark, exhibits a very distinctive feather pattern, making it easy to identify. The light gray feathers on its upper back and head contrast with the dark gray feathers on its wings and tail. It also has large white wing patches on the trailing edges of its wings.

These jays prefer stands of junipers and ponderosa pine, but can be found in coniferous forests extending up to treeline. A Clark's nutcracker can hold a large number of nuts in its beak and in a special pouch under its tongue. It hides the seeds, usually in the ground, and has the ability to locate its cached seeds when it's hungry.

Canada Jay *Perisoreus canadensis*

The Canada jay, officially known as the gray jay, also goes by the names whisky jack and camp robber. They have generally consistent, dark gray feathers on their backs with lighter feathers below, and are the smallest of the three jays common to the Rocky Mountains. All jays are members of the same family as crows, the *Corvidae* family. Birds from this family are the most common carriers of West Nile Virus.

Canada jays eat carrion, nuts, berries, and insects. They exhibit the interesting habit of gathering food and hiding it in trees. Using special mucous-secreting glands in the side of its beak, a Canada jay will glue together clumps of berries, nuts, and other food, which it will then stick to needles and branches. When times are tough, the jay returns to these caches of stored food. Canada jays are very bold birds, and will pick up food out of tents, off plates, and even off a hot charcoal grill.

Black-billed Magpie *Pica hudsonia*

The magpie, another member of the crow family, is found all over the Colorado Rockies. They have a very distinctive color pattern. Their bill, head, breast, and underside are black, while their belly, shoulders, and primary feathers are white. The wings and tail appear black, but on closer inspection they are an iridescent green.

Magpies prefer open, brush-covered country, but require trees for building their very large nests. They often belong to loose colonies of three to seven birds. If you are on the trail and you hear magpies, jays, or crows making a raucous noise, you can surmise that a bigger animal may be in the area. These birds tend to harass larger birds, bears, lions, coyotes, fox, and large snakes.

White-tailed Ptarmigan *Lagopus leucura*

Colorado's state bird is the lark bunting, but the ptarmigan would better represent the state because it is a year-round resident! The ptarmigan lives only in the high alpine regions of the state and does not migrate. The bunting, on the other hand, heads south to Texas

and Arizona when winter arrives.

Ptarmigan live on the windswept tundra during all four seasons. In the summer, the ptarmigan's plumage is the color of the rocks it lives amongst, making it difficult to see. In the winter, when most things are covered with snow, the ptarmigan has all white plumage.

The ptarmigan, a type of grouse, is well adapted for survival on the tundra. It survives by eating willows and other plants exposed by the blowing snow. Some people will read the name ptarmigan and mistakenly pronounce it "pete a mary gun." However, the "p" is silent and the name is pronounced "tar mee gun."

Mallard Duck *Anas platyrhynchos*

Mallard ducks are the most common wild ducks inhabiting Colorado's wetlands. The males are brightly colored and have a distinctive green head, a white collar, and a yellow bill. Like many birds, the females are mottled brown with a brown bill. Mallards will eat just about everything found in the wetlands, including insects, worms, slugs, snails, frogs, small crustaceans, grasses, and pond weeds. They build nests, usually on the ground, made of grass and leaves that they line with down. The drab, mottled coloration of females allows them to blend into their surroundings when nesting.

Male mallard

Female mallard

Male wood duck

Wood Duck *Aix sponsa*

The wood duck is, without a doubt, North America's most colorful duck. In fact, the scientific name means "waterbird in bridal dress." It's one of few North American ducks that nest in trees. The wood duck is a popular game bird.

The adult male is one of the most distinctive birds in the world and is difficult to describe. It has a very distinctive iridescent green, purple, tan, and blue plumage. Bright red eyes and a mostly red bill surrounded by face stripes make it stand out from other ducks. In contrast, the female is somewhat drab with grayish plumage and a white eye ring.

Enjoying Wildlife

Wildlife is a joy to watch, but animal's habits can change quickly due to the activity of humans. Approaching or feeding wildlife, for example, endangers humans as well as the wildlife. Animals will tend to flee rather than fight, but when they choose to defend themselves, man is generally the loser.

Feeding animals may seem to be something that will do no harm, but in reality, it significantly impacts their well-being. Our food products may not provide animals with the unique nutrients they need to survive. Therefore, wild animals that become dependant upon human food may suffer nutritional deficiencies. Animals, like bears, may find human food easier to obtain, but in time this will cause dangerous problems in the human community. Bears often become habituated to human food and will teach their young where that food can be found. This results in encounters between man and bears. Bears that become a problem or are considered a danger to public safety may be relocated or euthanized by the Colorado Division of Wildlife. Enjoy wildlife from a distance and do nothing that impacts their behavior or food habits. This will keep both you and the wildlife safe.

Bighorn Ram

Traveling in the High Country

As you travel the highways and byways of Colorado, you can do a number of things to protect and preserve this land for future generations. "Leave No Trace" is the best set of principles to follow. Do not litter or leave anything behind. The U.S. Forest Service says, "Pack it in, pack it out!" This simple solution saves thousands of tax dollars and maintains the pristine beauty of these mountains that we love.

When stopping at a trailhead, parking lot, or overlook, stay on the trails and avoid taking unmarked paths at the site. These shortcuts eventually add to the erosion and defacement of high-altitude terrain. This is particularly important in fragile areas like wetlands and alpine tundra. If leaving the established trail is necessary, walk a few hundred feet down the roadway before cutting across virgin ground. One trampling will generally not cause damage that cannot recover.

Antiquities Act

Throughout the West, hikers and travelers stumble upon ancient ruins, artifacts, and fossils. These historical remnants are fragile and irreplaceable. The Antiquities Act of 1906 protects them for the benefit of all Americans.

According to the act, any person who, without official permission, injures, destroys, excavates, or appropriates any historic or prehistoric ruin, artifact, or object of antiquity on the public lands of the United States is subject to arrest and penalty of law. Permits to

This wagon is typical of those that were used to haul supplies into Rocky Mountain mines in the 1800s.

excavate sites or remove artifacts can be issued only to recognized educational and scientific institutions.

"Enjoy but do not destroy your American Heritage!"

Stagecoaches and Wagon Roads

Colorado's Gold Rush began in 1859 and brought more people into the Rockies than ever before. Most traveled by foot or horseback, but there was a new demand for more efficient transportation. Entrepreneurs like Otto Mears seized this opportunity by building toll roads and creating transportation companies. At one time, forty-five stagecoach companies carried passengers and mail through Colorado's Rocky Mountains.

The stagecoaches, called Concord Stagecoaches, were drawn by teams of four or six horses. They got their name from the town where they were built: Concord, New Hampshire. Anyone who has seen a western movie has seen a Concord Stagecoach. Its popularity stemmed from its suspension system, which consisted of leather strapping called throughbraces supporting the coach. This design gave the stagecoaches a swinging motion, unlike wagons with leaf spring suspensions that bounced their cargo up and down.

A 1890s coach that traveled between Kremling and Denver.

These coaches were very popular in the East, and as rail travel increased the stagecoach manufacturers took their business West. Advertisements of the time touted fast coaches that could cover 2,500 miles in 70 days. Lucrative government mail contracts supplemented passenger revenue as financial backing for the purchase of such comfortable coaches.

Since there were no true windows on the wagons and coaches, the travelers had to endure the weather. Heat, cold, rain, and snow could only be countered by wearing appropriate clothing or using blankets and other covers. Dust from the horses added to the passenger's discomfort. Exceptionally rough roads, boggy areas, stream crossings without bridges, and stage robbers were realities of the time. Injured horses or equipment breakdowns might mean days of delay in the mountains, far from any town or shelter.

To smooth out the roadbed, "corduroy" roads were built in some areas. To make these roads, logs were laid across the roadway and covered with dirt. Imagine what a day or a week in a stagecoach would be like on those mountain roads. It often took *seven days* to travel from Leadville to Aspen over Independence Pass.

Still, stagecoaches operated in all weather conditions and, unbelievably, they continued to operate in the winter months. One could cross Independence Pass during the winter by stage in the late 1800s, but not by automobile today!

Stagecoach and wagon roads, like this one near Georgetown, were built over incredibly rough terrain. Rocks and timber were used to shore up the road and prevent if from collapsing.

All these thousands of miles of wagon roads through Colorado's mountains were built with hand labor—they didn't have bulldozers, trucks, or front-end loaders. Private individuals who built the roads recovered their construction costs by charging tolls at tollbooths placed at locations along the road that would be very difficult for travelers to circumvent.

Traveling in the Horseless Carriage

Even after cars began to replace carriages in the 1920s, travel was still not easy. Would you have called it an outing, an adventure, or an expedition to visit the mountains in your horseless carriage?

The roads were not yet well marked, if they were marked at all. None were even paved. To find out about the condition of the roadway, drivers relied on word of mouth, and even then, it was subject to major changes due to rockslides, rain, or washouts.

Maps that existed were very simple and often not to scale, making navigation even more of a challenge.

CONTINENTAL DIVIDE
TO THE ATLANTIC

A traveler on Berthoud Pass in 1917.

Gas was another issue. There was not a gas station at every major intersection, and if you did happen upon a station, there was no guarantee that they had gas. Most people that traveled strapped extra cans to their vehicle.

What if you needed help? There was no one to call and no way to make a call. If you had a flat or the car broke down, you had to fix the situation yourself. Most people who traveled by car took along tools, food, and other supplies. They packed for all kinds of weather, even if they only planned to be gone for a day or two. Drivers had to be pretty resourceful.

Gas Tax and Paving the High Roads

Colorado holds the distinction of being one of the first states to initiate a gasoline tax to fund roads. It all started in 1919 with a levy of $0.01 per gallon. During the New Deal of the 1930s, the number of miles of paved roads in Colorado quickly increased from 500 in 1930 to more than 4,000 in 1940. Because of the difficulty of constructing them, mountain passes were the last highways to be paved. It wasn't until 1931 that the state of Colorado paved the first pass over the Continental Divide—Berthoud Pass Toll Road, which soon became U.S. 40. Soon after, U.S. 50 over Monarch Pass was paved. The city of Denver began building a number of mountain touring roads, including the road to the top of Mount Evans. The Mount Evans road remains the highest road in the United States, reaching an elevation of over 14,000 feet.

So many roads began to appear in our nation during this time that a system was needed to help identify them on maps and in other documents. A group of federal and state officials met in Pinehurst,

North Carolina, on November 11, 1926, and developed a scheme that designated names for federal highways in all forty-eight states. The group assigned highways going east to west even numbers and highways going north to south odd numbers. All the major coast-to-coast highways received numbers ending with zero. Most states and counties now use similar strategies to identify roads.

Colorado Scenic and Historic Byways

Scenic Byway

A number of Colorado's spectacular highways carry a special designation: Colorado Scenic and Historic Byways. The Colorado Scenic and Historic Byways program identifies state roads of exceptional scenic beauty that provide recreational, educational, and economic benefits to the towns they pass through. Often, local boosters nominate a roadway, which must then receive its official designation from the Colorado Scenic and Historic Byways Commission.

An image of the Colorado state flower, the Columbine, on a white and blue sign marks these highways across the state. Nearby museums, chambers of commerce, or visitor centers usually offer free guides to Colorado's scenic and historic byways. You can find descriptions of each of the routes, as well as photos, maps, and the history of the areas along them at coloradobyways.org.

National Scenic Byways

AMERICA'S BYWAYS

The National Scenic Byways Program (NSBP) began making designations in 1991. Headed by the U.S. Secretary of Transportation, this program designates roads as National Scenic Byways or All-American Roads. They must demonstrate significant archaeological, cultural, historic, natural, recreational, or scenic qualities. Currently, 126 roads in 39 states hold this distinction. The Federal Highway Administration promotes these roads as America's Byways. Their website, byways.org, describes each of the routes. A sign with an image of a starred blue pennant on a white background marks these highways across the state.

The following highways, which carry one or both of the designations described above, cross passes included in this book.

Cache la Poudre-North Park
A Scenic Byway over Cameron Pass, 101 miles.

Guanella Pass
A Scenic Byway over Guanella Pass, parts are unpaved, 22 miles.

Los Caminos Antiguos
A Historic Byway over La Manga and Cumbres Passes, 129 miles.

Mount Evans
A Scenic Byway to the summit of Mount Evans, 28 miles.

San Juan Skyway **
A Scenic Byway over Molas Pass, Red Mountain Pass, and Dallas Divide, 236 miles.

Silver Thread
A Scenic Byway over Spring Creek and Slumgullion Passes, 75 miles.

Top of the Rockies **
A Scenic Byway over Fremont Pass and Independence Pass, 115 miles.

Trail Ridge Road **
A Scenic Byway over Milner Pass, 48 miles.

West Elk Loop
A Scenic Byway over Kebler Pass, 205 miles.

** National Scenic Byway

Driving Tips

The average automobile can traverse all the passes featured in this book. Some passes offer only dirt roads, but they are generally well-graded and easily traveled. This book does not include the many passes of Colorado that can only be accessed with a four-wheel-drive vehicle or on foot.

When traveling uphill in the mountains, be cautious that your car does not overheat. If the temperature light comes on or the gauges reach the red line, pull over, open the hood, and be patient and enjoy the scenery around you. Overheating can cause vapor lock or serious damage to the engine. If overheating is a common problem with your vehicle, take some preventative measures—turn off the air conditioning and, if possible, run the car in a low gear.

If a line of cars is building up behind you, pull over to let them pass. When following a slow car, remember that passing going uphill will take longer than average, and cars coming downhill may be going faster than average.

Top: Cattle guards are built along fence-lines where they cross a roadway. Cattle will not cross them because of the openings between the rails. Above: Fast-moving vehicles can be seriously damaged in collisions with cattle on open range.

In the fall, sheep are driven to pens near Colorado's high-country passes, such as this one on Red Mountain Pass. They used to be loaded onto trains for transportation, but now trucks are used.

When traveling downhill, save your brakes by putting the transmission into a lower gear to let the engine slow the vehicle down. Remember that it takes more distance to stop when traveling down a grade, and hot brakes are less efficient. In severe conditions, hot brakes can set a vehicle on fire.

Check weather forecasts, particularly in winter, before traveling, and learn how to drive in winter weather. Be sure to prepare your vehicle for those winter driving conditions—put on snow tires, pack tire chains, and bring along extra warm clothing and enough

Cowboys still drive cattle from horseback in much of Colorado's high country.

food and water to stay alive for a day or two. A breakdown can occur any time of day or night and in any weather condition.

Cell phone service is intermittent at best in the mountains. If a call is necessary, pull off the road at a spot where the signal quality is strong and stay in one location while making the call.

Driving on Open Range

Across the West, yellow signs warn of open range along roads and highways. Some show the silhouette of a cow or the words "Open Range." If a driver should hit livestock in open range, he carries responsibility for damage to his vehicle and for paying the rancher for the loss of his animal. If a driver is not in open range and hits livestock, the livestock owner bears responsibility for the damage to the vehicle and the loss of the livestock.

As population in the West grows, the idea of "home on the range" gets a lot more complicated. Laws related to open range have gotten increasingly more attention lately, and the litigation has shown that the public and the rancher don't see it the same way.

Wildlife and Roadways

Drivers in Colorado also need to be alert for wildlife on the roadways. Even though the roadways are often fenced, animals can go under, over, or through some of those fences. There are close to 1,000 animal-vehicle collisions that result in traffic fatalities or injuries in Colorado every year. Statistics on animal-vehicle collisions indicate that the average repair cost exceeds $2,000.

The Colorado State Patrol advises that when drivers encounter animals on the highway they should brake, but not attempt to swerve and avoid the animal. It's important to retain control of the vehicle before, during, and after a collision with an animal. Most fatalities and injuries occur because the driver loses control of the vehicle in a radical action to avoid hitting the animal. Drivers should be especially alert at dawn and dusk when animals are often on the move and difficult to see. At night, watch for their shining eyes.

Be alert for wildlife on the roadways.

High Altitude Safety

Many of Colorado's passes are above timberline, which creates a number of safety concerns that visitors may be unaware of or unprepared for. Please take the appropriate precautions to ensure personal safety.

Lightning

Lightning poses a deadly threat on high, exposed ridges. It can hit with a shock of one hundred million (or more!) volts, and is known to throw a person through the air, burn clothes, rupture eardrums, stop the heart from beating, and cause serious nervous disorders. If you see a storm nearby or hear thunder, head for the car and evacuate the area.

Altitude Sickness

At high elevations, the body does not work as well as it does at lower elevations because of the lack of oxygen. The following are all symptoms of altitude sickness:

- increased heart rate
- headache
- unusual tiredness
- problems sleeping
- shortness of breath
- nausea
- poor appetite

Some ways to avoid or reduce symptoms of altitude sickness are

On Mount Evans, ancient bristlecone pines, stripped and bent by prevailing winds, show the effects of the high country's brutal weather.

eating high-carbohydrate foods, drinking lots of water, using salt frugally, and avoiding alcoholic beverages. If you experience a worsening cough, shortness of breath while at rest, or fluid in the lungs, contact a doctor immediately. For many people, moving to a lower elevation quickly reduces adverse symptoms.

Hypothermia

Temperatures tend to drop as elevation increases, and weather in the high country can change quickly from hot and sunny to cold and snowing. Even a common afternoon rain shower can put a person who is unprepared in a life-threatening situation very quickly.

Hypothermia is a condition where the body's core temperature drops below that required for normal metabolism and bodily functions. This can occur even when temperatures do not reach freezing. Those who are wet, hungry, tired, or poorly dressed are especially at risk. The warning signs of hypothermia include:

- pale skin
- difficulty thinking or talking
- clumsiness
- irritability
- confusion
- quick, shallow breathing

If these symptoms occur, immediately take action to get the person warm and dry. To avoid hypothermia, pack lots of warm, insulating layers of clothing, and always be prepared for rain or snow. Try to avoid wearing cotton, which retains water, and avoid consuming alcohol.

Sunburn

Sunlight is more intense at higher elevations because of the thinner air. Even people with good tans are at risk for sunburn. Wear a high SPF sunscreen, even on foggy or cloudy days, to avoid sun damage. As little as twenty minutes of exposure can burn some people. To avoid eye damage and snow blindness, wear a hat and sunglasses or goggles.

Dehydration

Colorado commonly records humidity around 15 percent. The average afternoon relative humidity in the Midwest is from 60 percent to 85 percent! Many suggest that a person drink two to three times more water when at high elevations in order to make up for the increased amount of liquids lost to the dry air by breathing and sweating. But unless you're in a life-threatening situation, don't drink unfiltered water from streams or lakes. The water may appear clear, but microscopic parasites living in them can make a person very sick. Filtered water and juice are good choices to rehydrate, but tea, coffee, colas, and alcoholic beverages are not. Be aware that alcohol has an increased effect at higher altitudes.

Avalanche

Since 1950, avalanches have killed more people in Colorado than any other natural hazard, and Colorado accounts for one-third of all avalanche deaths in the United States. Large avalanches can bring down rocks and trees as well as snow, and can bury roadways for days and cause significant damage.

What causes an avalanche? Snowflakes tend to stick together when they reach the ground. The degree to which they stick varies considerably due to the temperature and moisture content of the air where the flakes form. If the pull of gravity exceeds the bonds between the flakes, the snow begins to move. Warm spells, rain, heavy snowstorms, or periods of strong wind may bring on ava-

Colorado Avalanche Information Center

The Colorado Avalanche Information Center (CAIC), which is in its twenty-second year of operation, is a program of the Colorado Geological Survey. Its goal is to minimize the impact of avalanches on the people and property of Colorado through a dual mission of forecasting and education. The CAIC reports more than 2,000 avalanches in an average winter. Thousands of people each year visit the CAIC website, http://avalanche.state.co.us, looking for avalanche information. CAIC personnel also present avalanche awareness talks and seminars across the state.

Avalanche professionals with experience in avalanche forecasting staff the information center at CAIC. They also monitor snow-pack, weather, and avalanche conditions in the mountains. The CAIC and other avalanche centers in the United States, Canada, and Europe publish a daily Avalanche Danger Scale.

lanches. In the spring, when snow becomes wet from thaw or rain, avalanche danger rises significantly. Snow on a steep slope may eventually develop a weak layer in the snow cover. Some kind of trigger, such as loud noises, wind, or travelers on skis or snowshoes, may be all that is needed to initiate an avalanche. Unstable snow cover can crack, collapse, or make hollow sounds.

In Colorado, the most avalanche-prone months are, in order, February, March, and January. Most avalanches occur on slopes of 25 to 50 degrees, on the down-wind side of a mountain, and above timberline. Avalanches may also run down gullies and small slopes below timberline, and can even travel through moderately dense forests. Most avalanches occur in the backcountry, out of sight and

away from developed areas. Bent or damaged trees show where avalanches have recently run.

The best way to survive an avalanche is to avoid it. A number of hotlines, mountain radio stations, and websites in Colorado provide information about current and forecasted weather, snow, and avalanche conditions. Travelers may find different conditions once they enter the backcountry, and they should know how to assess avalanche danger. Anyone venturing into avalanche country should carry special equipment, including an avalanche beacon, a shovel, and a collapsible probe or ski pole probe. Even practice with this equipment does not guarantee survival during an avalanche. Fewer than half of the people with beacons that have been buried in an avalanche actually survive. Statistics show that a fully buried avalanche victim who is still alive when the avalanche stops must be found and dug out within 15 minutes to have any reasonable chance of survival.

SnoTel Data Network

The SnoTel (Snowpack Telemetry) Data Network, managed by the National Water and Climate Center, collects real-time snow and climate data using automated, remote monitoring instruments. This data provides essential information to travelers, road maintenance workers, weather forecasters, wildland firefighters, ski area operators, mountaineers, and others. Hydrologists use the data to predict the spring runoff, thus forecasting the state's flood risks and determining the availability of water for irrigation and domestic use.

There are six hundred SnoTel remote sensing sites scattered across the mountains in eleven western states, including Alaska. Many are located atop mountain passes. They are often fenced as protection against livestock and wildlife. SnoTel sites are solar powered, with the solar panels mounted on a mast along with the antenna for radio transmission of data. They are designed to operate unattended and without maintenance for a year.

Every fifteen minutes, SnoTel sensors record and transmit information. The sites can also be remotely polled for data or directed to change the configuration of their sensors. The SnoTel website provides current and historical data, as well as analysis that is state or site specific. Data includes maps, tables, and graphs showing snow-water equivalent, snow depth, precipitation, temperature, wind speed/direction, relative humidity, and other climatic elements in hourly, daily, monthly, and yearly increments.

Some sites include "snow pillows." These bladders, filled with a fluid that measures the weight of the snow falling on top of them, convert that weight to snow-water equivalent, which helps hydrologists predict the spring runoff.

SnoTel uses one of the most advanced information transmission techniques—meteor burst communication technology—to transmit data via radio telemetry to a master station without using satellites. The term "meteor burst" refers to the way radio transmissions use ionized meteor trails 50 to 75 miles above the earth to bounce signals back to the master stations in Boise, Idaho, or Ogden, Utah. This technology allows the collection of data from the most remote locations. When the Boise and Ogden stations receive this data, they relay it to the National Water and Climate Center in Portland, Oregon.

Above: A SnoTel site on McClure Pass. Right: A SnoTel radio transmitter and rain, humidity, and temperature gauges.

SnoTel Sites Near Mountain Passes

Site Name	County
Cochetopa Pass	Saguache
Columbine Pass	Lower Gunnison
Fremont Pass	Summit
Hoosier Pass	Park
Independence Pass	Pitkin
Jones Pass	Grand
Lizard Head Pass	Dolores
Lynx Pass	Routt
McClure Pass	Pitkin
Medano Pass	Saguache
Molas Lake	Animas
Red Mountain Pass	Animas
Schofield Pass	Gunnison
Slumgullion	Hinsdale
Willow Creek Pass	Grand
Wolf Creek Summit	Mineral

Avalanche chute

Rabbit Ears Pass

Baker Mountain
8,824 feet
Mount of the Holy Cross
14,005 feet
Whiteley Peak
10,115 feet
Torreys Peak
14,267 feet
(See Mount Evans, pg. 82)
Mount Powell
13,560 feet
(See Vail Pass, pg. 92)
US 40
Dumont Lake
SE
S
73°

Rabbit Ears Pass has a false summit, so don't be fooled! Driving east from Steamboat Springs on US 40, you approach what appears to be the summit, but it is actually a high point at 9,400 feet. In the next 8 miles, the road descends a little, passing some beautiful alpine meadows along Walton Creek, then climbs again to reach the true summit of Rabbit Ears Pass. The highway crosses the Continental Divide here at 9,426 feet. Snowmobilers find easy access to the high country from Rabbit Ears Pass and use the area heavily

ORIGIN OF NAME	A nearby peak has a distinctive rabbit ears appearance.
ELEVATION	9,426 feet
NEARBY CITIES	Steamboat Springs/Kremmling
POINTS OF INTEREST	Muddy Pass, Old Rabbit Ears Pass
COUNTY	Jackson
HIGHWAY	US 40
MILEPOST	152.6
GPS	40°23'05"N by 106°36'42"W
TOPO MAP	Topo Map: Rabbit Ears Peak
GETTING THERE	**From Steamboat Springs,** head east on US 40 for 21 miles.
	From Kremmling, drive west on US 40 for 30 miles.

A variety of shrub species on the west side of Rabbit Ears Pass make fall a colorful season here.

in the winter months. When US 40 was extended over Berthoud and Rabbit Ears Passes, it became the first transmountain-transcontinental highway to provide year-round travel.

Blowdown

On October 25, 1997, a major wind event flattened approximately 20,000 acres of trees 20 miles north of Rabbit Ears Pass. On that same day, a blizzard buried the plains of eastern Colorado, and winds literally flattened 31 square miles of old-growth trees in Routt National Forest.

Spruce bark beetle larvae survive the winter by metabolizing an alcohol that acts as antifreeze.

The extent of the blowdown near Rabbit Ears wasn't discovered until foresters doing an aerial survey flew over the area days after the storm passed. It appeared to the foresters that a giant had stepped on the 100-foot tall, 200- to 350-year-old trees. They were all blown down to the west, against the normal west to east wind flow. It's estimated that the winds that flattened these trees may have reached 150 mph.

The howling windstorm trapped many hunters in the area, some of whom literally chain-sawed their way out of the woods. The storm system dumped a tremendous amount of snow on the Front Range, but left no snow on the area of the blowdown.

Many of the blown down trees could be salvaged through logging, but 12,000 acres were inside the Mount Zirkel Wilderness and off-limits to timber harvesting. A massive infestation of spruce bark beetles feasted on the felled timber the following summer.

Lupine and Indian paintbrush frame 10,654-foot Rabbit Ears Peak.

Downhill to a Summit?

Travel about 3.5 miles east of Rabbit Ears Pass on US 40 to reach one of the most interesting passes in Colorado: Muddy Pass. Also on the Continental Divide, it is the only pass in the state where two major roadways converge at the summit of a pass, and you reach it by driving downhill! The summit is at the junction of CO 14 and US 40. Proceeding south on US 40 takes you to the town of Kremmling, and proceeding north on Colorado 14 takes you to the town of Walden. Within the Muddy Pass/Rabbit Ears Pass area, US 40 crosses the Continental Divide twice in 2 miles, and it crosses three counties (Routt, Grand, and Jackson) within 6 miles.

Steamboat Springs

On the west side of Rabbit Ears Pass is the town of Steamboat Springs. According to local lore, the town got its name from three French fur trappers who traveled down the Yampa River in 1865. One of them heard what sounded like the chugging of a paddle-wheel steamer. What was actually making the noise was a bubbling mineral spring, just one of 150 known in the area. They named the area Steamboat Springs, and the name stuck.

Steamboat claims something no other community can. Since 1932, Steamboat has produced sixty-nine Winter Olympians, more

Above: Flower garden at the summit of Cameron Pass; Top left: Blue columbine; Top right: Pink plumes

than any other town in the United States, and has sent athletes to all but two winter games.

Howelsen Hill, on the south side of Steamboat, is Colorado's oldest ski area that is still in operation. It opened in 1915 and is named for Carl Howelsen, a Norwegian skier who lived in Steamboat. The city of Steamboat Springs owns and manages Howelsen Hill. Steamboat's larger resort, Mt. Werner, opened in 1963 under the name Storm Mountain. It was renamed when Steamboat lost its hometown hero, Olympic skier Buddy Werner, after he died in an avalanche in Switzerland on April 12, 1964. In 1969 the area became known as Steamboat Ski Area.

Steamboat's Winter Carnival, hosted yearly since 1914, is the longest running winter carnival west of the Mississippi. The carnival started with cross-country ski races and ski jumping competitions, and now includes skijoring races, where horses pull skiers. Other carnival attractions include a film festival, dual slalom bicycle race, snowboarding, and the Steamboat Springs High School band on skis.

Cameron Pass

Looking south from Cameron Pass. The peaks on the left are in Rocky Mountain National Park.

Iron Mountain
12,265 feet
E
Thunder Mountain
12,060 feet
Lulu Mountain
12,228 feet
Nokhu Crags
12,485 feet
(See **Milner Pass,** pg. 50)
S
Upper Michigan Ditch
Seven Utes Mountain
11,453 feet
224°

Cameron Pass, located about 55 miles west of Fort Collins on CO 14, is the northern-most pass on the Colorado State Highway map. Total traffic over this pass does not rival that over other passes in the state because it does not connect any major cities. No ski areas or tourist destinations exist in the region, and the area around the pass is dominated by Colorado State Forest and Roosevelt National Forest lands. Many people who enjoy the beauty of the area around Cameron Pass appreciate these facts.

ORIGIN OF NAME	Discovered by General R. A. Cameron, founder of Fort Collins
ELEVATION	10,276 feet
NEARBY CITIES	Walden, Ft Collins
POINTS OF INTEREST	Nokhu Crags; the Colorado State Forest; Walden, the "Moose Viewing Capital of Colorado"
COUNTY	Larimer
HIGHWAY	C0 14/ Cache La Poudre-North Park Scenic and Historic Byway
MILEPOST	64.8
GPS	40°31'15"N by 105°53'33"W
TOPO MAP	Clark Peak
GETTING THERE	**From Walden,** travel east on CO 14 for 30 miles to the summit.

Several tribes of American Indians can claim to be the first human inhabitants of the Cameron Pass area. Though Ute, Crow, and Sioux bands all roamed through the area, the Arapaho and Cheyenne dominated this part of Colorado in the nineteenth century.

With the discovery of silver just southwest of Cameron Pass in the 1870s, Teller City, a mining camp, became the first major town in the area and in the Never Summer mountain range. A 100-mile toll road, completed in 1882 by the Cache La Poudre and North Park Toll Road Company, served as the first road over the pass, connecting Fort Collins to Teller. Road improvements and construction continued, and by 1927 an automobile could travel from Fort Collins to Walden via Cameron Pass. Convict labor provided much of the construction.

Adult moose are 6 to 7 feet tall and can weigh up to 1,600 pounds. They are the second largest land-animal in North America. Bison are the largest.

The highway over Cameron Pass saw new improvements in the 1970s when developers proposed a plan to build a ski area on the pass. This plan was in response to a state bid to host the Winter Olympics in Colorado. Environmentalists and a statewide vote derailed the Olympic bid, and the ski area was never built. The road, however, was paved as part of the original development plan.

Nokhu Crags

The Nokhu Crags, located just outside the northwest corner of Rocky Mountain National Park, are visible to the west of Cameron Pass. The Arapaho Indians named them *nea ha-noXhu,* meaning eagle's nest, but the locals later shortened the name to Nokhu. The crags began to form millions of years ago when shale layers were exposed to extreme

Moose sculpture made of barbed wire at the Colorado State Forest Office near the town of Gould.

Moose Viewing Capital of Colorado

Moose are not considered indigenous to Colorado. In 1978, the Colorado Division of Wildlife (DOW) introduced 12 moose into North Park, about 15 miles west of Cameron Pass. These were the first moose ever introduced into Colorado. It is estimated that there are now more than 600 moose in North Park, and the number in the state may be in the thousands. As evidence of the success of the introductions, the state legislature designated the town of Walden the "Moose Viewing Capital of Colorado" in 1995. For more about moose, see page 17.

heat and compression. These forces converted the shale into hornfels, a hard, erosion-resistant rock that tends to be brittle and easily broken. When plate tectonic activity formed the Rocky Mountains, the hornfels lifted up along with the shale that surrounded it. Erosion eventually wore down the shale, leaving the dramatic mountain and rock formations seen from Colorado State Highway 14.

Railroad Ties

The forests around Cameron Pass provided much of the timber that the Transcontinental Railroad used for railroad ties. The men who made these ties were called tie hacks. A really good tie hack could cut thirty to forty ties a day, all by hand. Typical pay was ten cents per tie.

Tie hacks worked throughout the year, enduring freezing winters and difficult living conditions. Every spring from 1870 to 1910, a tie drive was implemented to transport the ties from the forests near the pass to the town of La Porte, about 65 miles to the east. The tie hacks stacked the ties along the Cache La Poudre River until spring thaw came. Then they threw them in and let them float downstream to La Porte. Inevitably, the ties would jam, requiring the drivers to dislodge them, sometimes with dynamite, to keep them moving. A tie drive was cold, dangerous work.

Aspen leaf

Widespread harvesting of the forests for ties almost destroyed them. However, thanks to the restoration work of Colorado State University in Fort Collins and the U.S. Forest Service, today you can hardly tell where the cutting occurred when traveling over Cameron Pass.

Colorado State Forest

In 1876, when Colorado was granted statehood, the federal government granted in trust to the new state approximately 4.5 million acres of land for the purpose of generating revenues to support state schools. Because this land was divided into small, separated sections, many exchanges occurred to create larger contiguous blocks of land.

In 1938, a land exchange between the Colorado State Board of Land Commissioners and the United States Forest Service created the 70,980-acre parcel of land that the Colorado legislature designated as the Colorado State Forest. The legislature required that the Colorado State Land Board "provide for and extend the practice of ... forestry" in the state forest. The land board assumed responsibility for managing the grazing, recreation, and forestry on state forest land.

The land board oversaw timber harvesting in the state forest from 1940 to 1970. Several large logging camps operated in the forest, including the largest in Colorado history, the Bockman Lumber Camp. At one point, this camp employed over one hundred men and their families, all of whom lived at the camp. In the mid-sixties, timber harvesting in the state forest began to meet public controversy due to its levels and visibility, resulting in the closure of all logging camps there by the early seventies.

In 1971, the Colorado Division of Parks and Outdoor Recreation assumed responsibility for managing recreation in the forest. A grazing association now manages the livestock use of the forest, leaving the state land board with the sole responsibility of forest management.

Milner Pass

View looking out from the Gore Range Overlook on Trail Ridge Road. This is a 200° panorama.

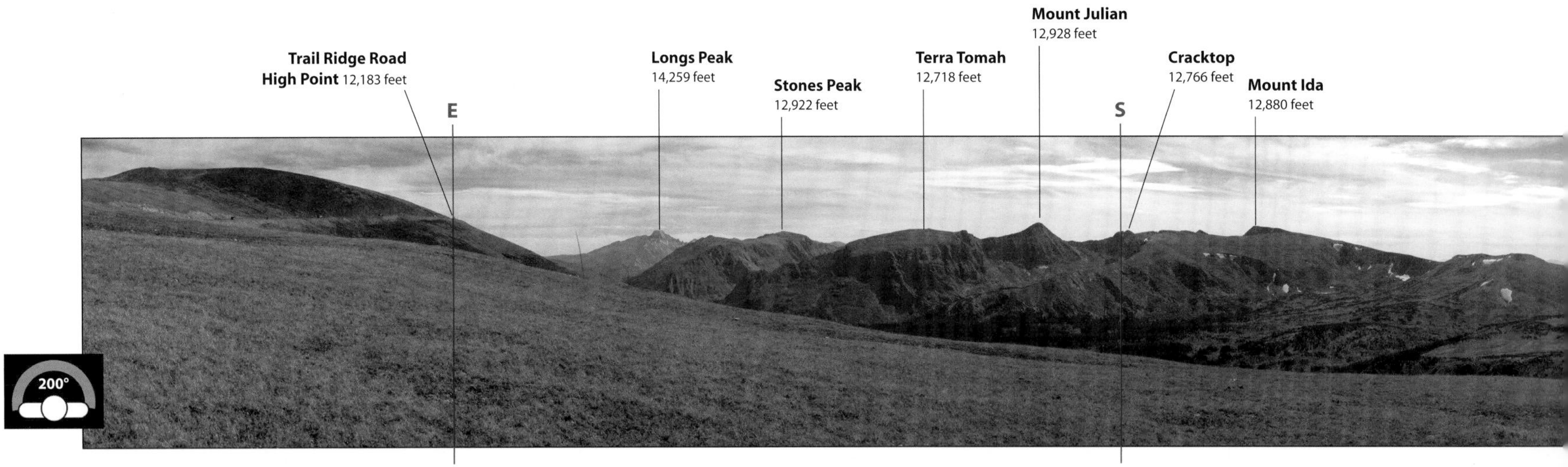
Trail Ridge Road
High Point 12,183 feet
E
Longs Peak
14,259 feet
Stones Peak
12,922 feet
Terra Tomah
12,718 feet
Mount Julian
12,928 feet
S
Cracktop
12,766 feet
Mount Ida
12,880 feet
200°

continued on next page

Milner Pass, seated on the Continental Divide, is located on scenic Trail Ridge Road in Rocky Mountain National Park. Nearby Estes Park has been a popular tourist destination since the early 1900s. There is plenty of history and high mountain majesty to explore when venturing to Milner Pass.

Highest Paved Highway in the USA

Trail Ridge Road, part of transcontinental US 34, crosses Milner Pass on the Continental Divide at 10,758 feet. Though the pass

ORIGIN OF NAME	Surveyed by T .J. Milner, a railroad engineer who was looking for a route from Denver to Salt Lake City.
ELEVATION	10,758 feet
NEARBY CITIES	Grand Lake/Estes Park
POINTS OF INTEREST	Stanley Hotel, Rocky Mountain National Park, Longs Peak
COUNTY	Grand
HIGHWAY	US 34/Trail Ridge Road
MILEPOST	16.3
GPS	40°25'11"N by 105°48'41"W
TOPO MAP	Rocky Mountain National Park or Forest Canyon Pass
GETTING THERE	**From Granby,** drive north on US 34 for 16 miles to Grand Lake. Continue north on US 34 towards Estes Park for another 18 miles. **From Estes Park,** travel west on US 34 for 21 miles to the summit.

continued from previous page

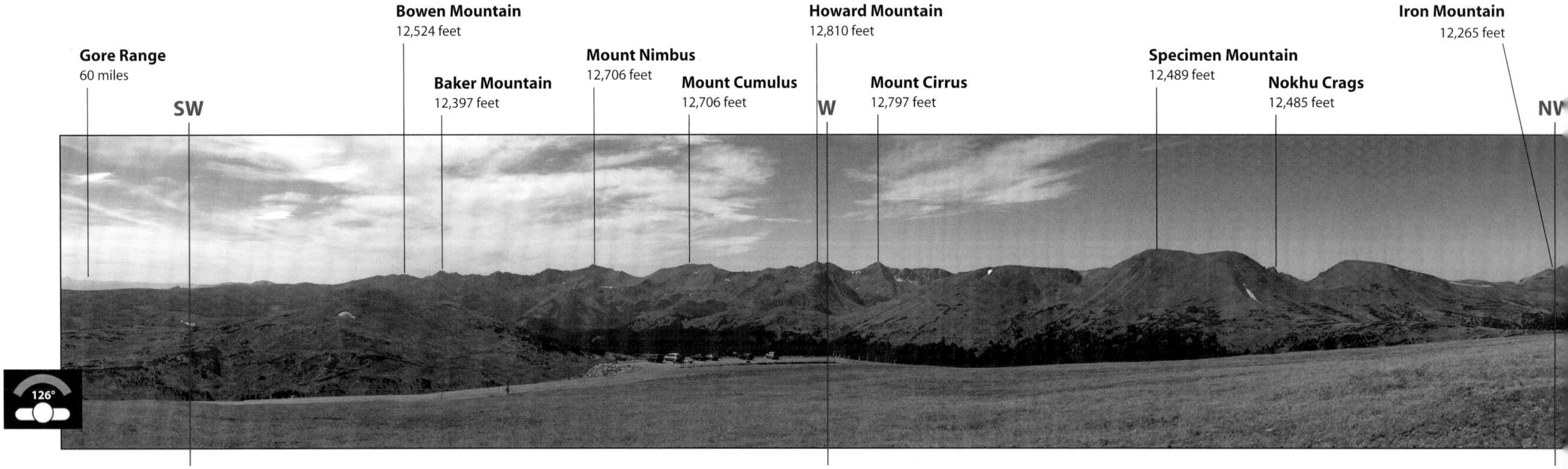
Gore Range
60 miles
Bowen Mountain
12,524 feet
Baker Mountain
12,397 feet
Mount Nimbus
12,706 feet
Mount Cumulus
12,706 feet
Howard Mountain
12,810 feet
Mount Cirrus
12,797 feet
Specimen Mountain
12,489 feet
Nokhu Crags
12,485 feet
Iron Mountain
12,265 feet
SW
W
NW
126°

itself does not offer any spectacular vistas, a 6-mile drive east to where the road winds above treeline will reveal some of the most dramatic high-mountain views found anywhere in the United States. At this point, about 29 miles west of Estes Park and 18 miles east of Grand Lake, Trail Ridge Road/US 34 reaches a high point of 12,183 feet, making it the highest continuously paved highway in the United States.

Due to wind-blown winter snows, Trail Ridge Road is closed from just after Labor Day to just before Memorial Day each year.

Trail Ridge Road

Clearing the road for its annual opening ceremony takes about thirty-five days of plowing. Huge rotary plows cut their way through snow banks up to 20 feet deep.

Archeological records show that humans have lived in the Estes Park area for at least 12,000 years.

Estes Park

In 1859, Joel Estes entered a beautiful valley east of what is today Rocky Mountain National Park while hunting with his son. He decided to settle there, and returned the next summer to build several log structures. Estes brought his family to the valley in the summer of 1863. Though Estes only stayed in the area for six years, the town still carries his name. Griffith J. "Griff" Evans, a Welshman, obtained the Estes property and provided the first tourist accommodations in the area. Estes Park has since grown into a popular tourist destination.

Poudre Lake. Trail Ridge Road and the parking area for Milner Pass are visible in the right-hand corner.

The Stanley Hotel

In 1907, F. O. Stanley began construction on the now world-famous Stanley Hotel. Some of the timber used to construct the hotel came from the Bear Lake fire of 1900. Many say they can still smell a faint odor of wood smoke on a warm summer day. Well known for its architecture and spectacular setting, the Stanley gained more recent attention after it played a role in the movie version of Stephen King's novel, *The Shining*. It has now become what many consider to be one of America's most haunted hotels.

Enos Mills

Enos Mills bought the Lamb Ranch in 1902, and in 1904 changed the name to Longs Peak Inn. Mills was a naturalist and used the inn as a place to acquaint his guests with the natural world. He became well

A cold, late-fall day at Lake Irene near Milner Pass.

View from the Grand Lake Lodge. Grand Lake is on the left and Shadow Mountain Lake is on the right. The town between them is Grand Lake.

known for his naturalist activities, his many books about the natural history of the area, and for reportedly climbing Longs Peak 304 times. However, Mills is best known for being the "Father of Rocky Mountain National Park."

A New National Park

In 1909, Enos Mills proposed that a national park named The Estes National Park and Game Preserve be established in this spectacular area of the Colorado Rockies. In his vision, the park would extend all the way from the Mummy Range, past Longs Peak, and down to Mt. Evans. Many locals, the Denver Chamber of Commerce, and the Colorado Mountain Club supported the concept. The cumbersome name finally morphed into Rocky Mountain National Park, and the boundaries of the park were hotly contested.

The first official proposal for the park, prepared by Robert B. Marshall, Chief Geographer of the U.S. Geological Survey at the time, had it covering more than 700 square miles and encompassing not only the Estes Park area but also Indian Peaks to the south. After two years of hard work and a lot of compromise, the Senate finally passed a final version of the bill. On January 26, 1915, President Wilson signed the bill, making Rocky Mountain National Park a reality.

Today, Rocky Mountain National Park is considered one of the most spectacular high-mountain areas in North America. The 415-square-mile park ranges in elevation from 8,000 feet to 14,259 feet at the summit of Longs Peak. Hikers and climbers enjoy 359 miles of trail and 60 peaks over 12,000 feet.

Longs Peak and its neighbor Mount Meeker are sometimes referred to as the Twin Peaks.

The Never Summer Range, viewed from Trail Ridge Road.

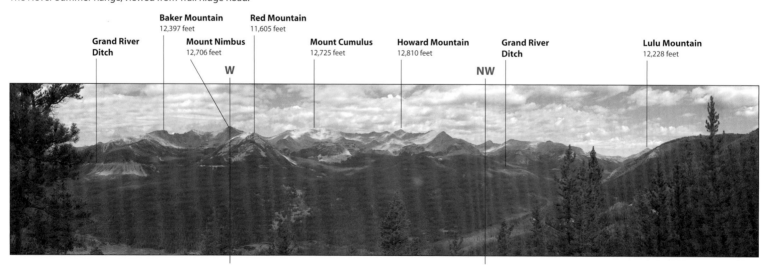

Grand River Ditch
Baker Mountain 12,397 feet
Mount Nimbus 12,706 feet
W
Red Mountain 11,605 feet
Mount Cumulus 12,725 feet
Howard Mountain 12,810 feet
NW
Grand River Ditch
Lulu Mountain 12,228 feet

The Great Circle Tour

Roe Emery, later called "The Father of Colorado Tourism," pioneered the "Great Circle Tour," an easy, affordable, and breathtaking bus tour of the central Colorado Rockies. Tourists would start from Union Station in Denver and arrive at the Estes Park Chalet for dinner and a night's lodging. The next day, the bus would travel up the switchbacks of Trail Ridge Road, over the high point the tour company called "The Top of the World," and down to the town of Grand Lake for the night. Guests dined on Grand Lake Lodge's huge deck, where they could enjoy an impressive view of the town's namesake—the largest natural lake in Colorado. After breakfast, the bus traveled south through Middle Park and over Berthoud Pass, with a stop in Idaho Springs to enjoy hot springs, dinner, and a good night's sleep at The Hot Springs Hotel. The following day, the bus returned to Denver.

Roads through Rocky Mountain National Park

The original road into Rocky Mountain National Park followed the Fall River to 11,796-foot Fall River Pass. Fall River Road, completed in 1920, continues to be popular with park visitors who enjoy navigating its many tight hairpin curves. Now a one-way, uphill, dirt road, Fall River Road provides the visitor with a first-hand understanding of what mountain roads were like in the 1920s.

The original Fall River Road was rough, steep, and didn't make for a very scenic drive. Views from Trail Ridge, a mountain ridge to the south, were far superior, and a plan to construct a road there soon evolved. Construction of Trail Ridge Road began in September, 1929, and was completed by July, 1932.

Fall River Road follows a route used long ago by American Indian hunters

This was not a normal road construction project. The weather permitted only four to five months of construction a year, and protection of the surrounding environment was a high priority. Contractors worked feverishly but carefully with tractors, graders, horses, and gas-powered steam shovels. Log and rock dikes along the roadway minimized damage to rock walls during blasting. Stonemasons placed surface rocks lichen-side up and salvaged tundra sod to replace along the roadway. They used rocks from the surroundings to build guardrails along the shoulder of the road. All of this produced an aesthetic experience unlike that of any other roadway in Colorado.

Trail Ridge Road ended at Fall River Pass where it met Fall River Road. Fall River Road was not suitable for automobile traffic until 1938.

Rocky's Highest Peak

At 14,259 feet, Longs Peak is the highest mountain in Rocky Mountain National Park. Its square-shaped top, as viewed from Trail Ridge Road, gives it an identity that cannot be mistaken. The mountain gained some notoriety in 1866 when Jules Verne named it as the fictional site for a 280-foot telescope in the movie *From the Earth to the Moon*. Today, it is one of Colorado's favorite fourteeners, and its steep east face, known as The Diamond, makes it especially popular with technical rock climbers.

The peak carries the name of Stephen Long, who explored the Rocky Mountain National Park area in 1820. John Wesley Powell and newspaperman William Byers led the first recorded ascent of Longs Peak on August 23, 1868. Most people now climb the peak from the east, but Powell and Byers made the ascent from the Grand Lake side. They were probably not the first to climb the peak; Arapaho Indians also speak of summiting Longs.

Reverend Elkanah J. Lamb established a new route up Longs Peak in 1871, but he's more famous for the way he got down. He descended a couloir, now called Lamb's Slide, on the mountain's east side in a not-so-graceful manner—on the seat of his pants.

Climbing Longs Peak became increasingly popular, and in 1925 two sets of cables were affixed to the mountain's north face on what is now called the Cable Route. These cables assisted hikers in ascending what was then a popular route up the mountain. Two years later a cabin was built in the Boulder Field. Climbers sometimes traveled to the cabin on horseback, stayed the night, and undertook the final ascent the following day. The cabin was used regularly until 1937, when it was abandoned. The park service removed the cables and the cabin in 1973.

Today, most people ascend Longs by the Keyhole route. It is about 8 miles one-way to the summit, has an elevation gain of 4,850 feet, and is the only non-technical route up the mountain.

Every year more than 4,000 people hike or climb to Longs' summit. Thousands of others start the trip but turn back because of inclement weather or their own lack of physical ability. In the summer, afternoon storms often bring heavy rain, thunder, and lightning. Winter storms can be far worse. Hikers and climbers must understand the dangers of their attempt before they proceed. More than fifty people have lost their lives on Longs Peak. Climbing Longs can be a rewarding experience for those who are prepared, but neither climbers nor hikers should underestimate the difficulty of ascending this rugged mountain.

Different maps place Longs Peak at 14,255 or 14,259 feet. The U.S. Geological Survey improved cartographic accuracy in 2002 and set the official heights of many Colorado landmarks as much as 7 feet higher than before. Longs' "official" height is now 14,259 feet.

Left: Longs Peak viewed from Trail Ridge Road; Above: Another view of Longs Peak.

Berthoud Pass

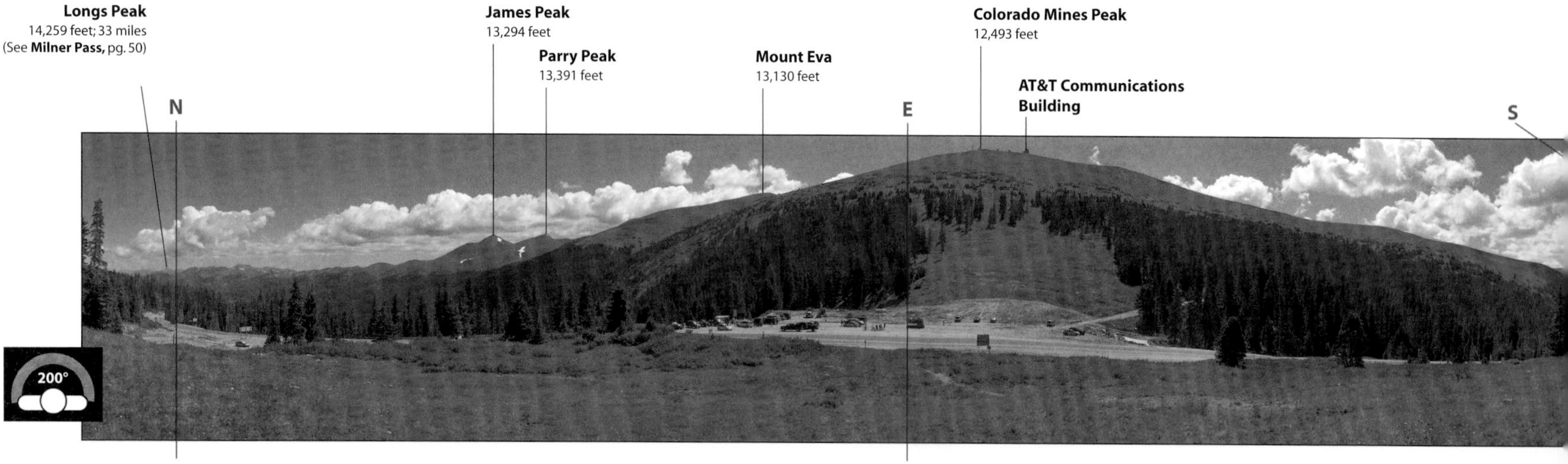
Longs Peak
14,259 feet; 33 miles
(See Milner Pass, pg. 50)
James Peak
13,294 feet
Parry Peak
13,391 feet
Mount Eva
13,130 feet
Colorado Mines Peak
12,493 feet
AT&T Communications Building
N
E
S
200°

Every year, thousands of skiers and snowboarders cross **Berthoud Pass** on their way to Winter Park and Steamboat Springs. Located on US 40 about 55 miles west of Denver, the summit of the pass is at 11,315 feet. Reaching it requires negotiating a steep grade with many switchbacks. The pass rewards drivers with many sweeping views of the Colorado Rockies. Outdoor adventurers seek out Berthoud Pass for its backcountry skiing access and Continental Divide Trail trailhead.

ORIGIN OF NAME	Captain Edward L. Berthoud discovered the pass while looking for railroad routes through the Rockies.
ELEVATION	11,315 feet
NEARBY CITIES	Winter Park/Idaho Springs
POINTS OF INTEREST	Moffat Tunnel, Continental Divide National Scenic Trail, Rollins Pass, Georgetown Loop Railroad
COUNTY	Clear Creek
HIGHWAY	US 40
MILEPOST	243
GPS	39°47'54"N by 105°46'40"W
TOPO MAP	Berthoud Pass
GETTING THERE	From **Winter Park,** travel east on US 40 for 11 miles to the summit. From **near Idaho Springs** on I 70, take exit 232 and drive west on US 40 for 15 miles.

View from near Berthoud Pass.

The First Paved Highway Over the Continental Divide

The Colorado Central Railroad Company facilitated the discovery of Berthoud Pass when they were looking for routes over the Rockies. When the company's secretary and chief engineer, Captain Edward L. Berthoud, attempted a route over the pass in 1861, he determined that it would be suitable for a wagon road, but not a railroad. A wagon road was built over the pass in 1874, and by the 1920s it was drivable with automobiles. The state bought the road in 1931. When they paved it in 1938, US 40 became the first paved highway in Colorado to cross the Continental Divide. US 40 opened up many towns in Middle Park to tourists, and it's still the best way to access Winter Park and Steamboat Springs.

Skiing at Berthoud Pass

The Berthoud Pass Ski Area, which opened in 1937, was one of the first major ski areas in Colorado. The original permit for the ski area, granted by the U.S. Forest Service, included over 37,000 acres on both sides of the pass and encompassed parts of the current Winter Park

Bare-what?

Edward L. Berthoud's native Swiss countrymen pronounce his name "bare-too," but both Berthoud Pass and the town of Berthoud, Colorado, which were named after him, are pronounced locally as "burr-thud."

Resort. In 1947, they installed the first double chairlift in Colorado, only a year after the world's first double chairlift was installed in Oregon's Hoodoo Ski Area. According to a 1938 U.S. Forest Service booklet, an estimated one-third of all Colorado skiers frequented Berthoud Pass in those early years. Later, Berthoud Pass became the first Colorado ski area to allow snowboarders full access to lifts and terrain.

The competition of larger ski areas eventually forced Berthoud Pass Ski Area to close on March 10, 2003. Its forest service permit required that all remaining structures be removed, and in the summer of 2005 the lodge and other buildings were torn down. In 2008, a new warming hut was opened at the summit. This eco-friendly hut accommodates up to eighty people and is heated with passive solar and radiant heat. It includes minimal restrooms equipped with composting toilets. Parking for Berthoud Pass was expanded at the time of construction; the new lot can accommodate 120 cars.

Now that Berthoud Pass Ski Area is closed, skiers use the area in the same fashion that they did before it originally opened. Before 1937, skiers drove cars to the top of the 11,315-foot pass and skied down to the bottom, where they loaded into cars to head back to the top. They also hiked up the mountains above the top parking lot to reach areas above treeline. Today, Berthoud is once again a popular destination for backcountry skiers.

The Continental Divide National Scenic Trail

The Continental Divide National Scenic Trail (CDNST) crosses Berthoud Pass, making this site an important trailhead location for access to the CDNST in Colorado. The pass also offers one of the

View from near the top of the old Berthoud Pass Ski Area.

few paved access points to this trail, which is possibly why it is one of the most visited CDNST trailheads in the United States.

The dream of a trail following the Continental Divide began becoming a reality in 1978 when Congress designated 3,100 miles stretching from Canada to Mexico as a National Scenic Trail. The trail, which was approximately 70 percent complete as of 2008, courses through five states and some of the nation's most spectacular scenery. It would be impossible to actually walk the divide in some places, so the trail follows existing trails in nearby areas to follow the divide as closely as is practical. The trail crosses the divide at the following passes: Rabbit Ears Pass (pg. 40), Berthoud Pass (pg. 62), Monarch Pass (pg. 166), Stony Pass, Wolf Creek Pass (pg. 224) and Cumbres Pass (pg. 230). The trail also comes near many other passes in the state.

MOFFAT
TUNNEL
1923
1927
5595
5595
40

A Union Pacific coal train emerges from the west portal of the Moffat Tunnel.

The Ski Train

Those not wishing to drive their cars over Berthoud can avoid the pass with the Ski Train. The Ski Train began its regular, scheduled trips to Winter Park Resort in 1940. The trip continues to be very popular, partly because the train stops less than 100 yards from Winter Park's ski lifts. Today, the train uses fourteen passenger cars to transport 750 passengers at a time, the largest capacity of any scheduled passenger train in the United States.

After leaving Denver and traveling past the towns of Pinecliff and Rollinsville, the route climbs about 4,000 feet and passes through 29 tunnels. The total travel time for the 57-mile ride is a little over two hours—about the same amount of time it would take to make the trip from Denver to Winter Park by car, given good driving conditions.

A trip on the Ski Train is rewarded by convenience, camaraderie, and beautiful scenery. Returning at night to Denver's sparkling city lights is especially remarkable, and there are no sloppy roads or traffic to contend with after a long day on the slopes.

The Ski Train doesn't pass over the Continental Divide—it drives under it! Skiers riding on the train often make bets on the amount of time to the nearest second it will take the train to pass through the historic, 6.2-mile-long Moffat Tunnel. In the event that you are in the pool, it takes an average of twelve minutes!

Members and volunteers with a nonprofit group, the Continental Divide Trail Alliance (CDTA), work to construct, manage, and preserve the trail. The trail is designed for foot and horse travel, but bikes are permitted on some sections.

The trail crosses twenty-five national forests, thirteen wilderness areas, three national parks, one national monument, eight BLM areas, and the states of Montana, Idaho, Wyoming, Colorado, and New Mexico. A total of 760 miles of the CDNST cross Colorado. It reaches an elevation of 14,270 feet—the high point of the trail in the U.S.—at the summit of Grays Peak, just east of Loveland Pass (pg. 70). Since the trail roughly follows the divide, it offers a rugged, backcountry experience.

The Mines Electronic Site

Berthoud Pass hosts the Mines Peak Electronic Site, an important transcontinental communication link. Inaugurated in 1959, the site

Transmission towers on the summit of 12,493-foot Mines Peak near Berthoud Pass.

now includes many towers for electronic data and phone transmissions. AT&T and Qwest are two of the companies that have towers here.

A dirt road provides access to the structures from US 40. Maintenance personnel must rely on snowmobiles and snowcats for winter access. The high elevation of this site—it sits above the pass at 12,493 feet—is desirable because the signal must travel in a straight line for up to 40 miles to reach towers located on other high peaks. By placing the towers on a peak, the physical height of the towers can be minimized while maximizing the distance between towers.

Loveland Pass

View from the Loveland Pass parking area.

Hager Mountain
13,195 feet
Pettingell Peak
13,553 feet
Mount Sniktau
13,234 feet
Loveland
Ski Area
I-70 Eisenhower
Tunnel
W
N
US 6
180°

US 6 crosses **Loveland Pass** at an elevation of 11,990 feet and provides the traveler with some very spectacular views. Since the opening of the Eisenhower Memorial Tunnel in 1973, fewer travelers use Loveland Pass. Going through the tunnel rather than over Loveland Pass saves a driver 9.5 miles and a half an hour of time, but they miss out on the views!

W.A. Loveland lends his name to this famous Colorado pass located 60 miles west of Denver. He gained his fortune as a railroad entrepreneur and businessman, but he also founded the city of Golden and convinced the Colorado Territorial Legislature to establish the Colorado School of Mines in his city.

Unable to extend his railroad line, the Colorado Central Railroad, over the pass, Loveland built a wagon road across it in 1879. In the 1930s Charles Vail, the state highway engineer, converted the wagon road into an automobile highway. It was paved in 1950.

Driving over Loveland Pass was, and still is, a challenge, particularly in winter when avalanches frequently close the road. Large trucks trying to make it up the steep grade often slow traffic on the 9.5-mile, two-lane road.

Avoiding a Pass

With the passage of time, Loveland Pass became a bottleneck for travelers trying to get from Denver to destinations west of there. By the 1960s, I-70 reached the base of Loveland Pass with nowhere to go. The Interstate needed a divided highway with two lanes in each direction, and Loveland Pass was not the solution. Even though a number of railroad engineers had unsuccessfully attempted to tunnel at this location, highway engineers devised a new, audacious plan to construct a 1.7-mile tunnel under the Continental Divide, enabling them to bypass Loveland Pass all together.

ORIGIN OF NAME	Named for W.A. Loveland, a railroad entrepreneur and businessman
ELEVATION	11,992 feet
NEARBY CITIES	Silverthorne/Georgetown
POINTS OF INTEREST	Eisenhower Tunnel, Arapahoe Basin Ski Area, Lake Dillon
COUNTY	Summit
HIGHWAY	US 6
MILEPOST	225
GPS	39°39'49"N by 105°52'45"W
TOPO MAP	Loveland Pass
GETTING THERE	**From Silverthorne,** travel east on US 6 for 16 miles. **From Georgetown,** drive west on I-70 and take exit 216. Continue south on US 6 for 17 miles.

Looking down on the Loveland Pass parking area.

Construction of the tunnel, to be called the Eisenhower Memorial Tunnel, began on March 15, 1968. Four companies worked for five years to complete the first of the twin bores under the Continental Divide. The effort required more than a thousand laborers year-round. The second bore was completed in 1979.

The tunnel immediately created a huge economic impact on western Colorado and its ski areas. Travelers not only could avoid the dangerous drive and thick traffic over Loveland Pass, but also saved time and money as well. Even though the Eisenhower Tunnel eliminates a difficult and sometimes dangerous drive, the approaches to the tunnel may still be treacherous when winter driving conditions exist.

The Eisenhower Tunnel during construction.

A Really Big Operation

The elevation at the east entrance to the Eisenhower Tunnel is 11,012 feet, and the west entrance is at 11,158 feet, making it the highest vehicular tunnel in the world. Where the tunnel crosses the

West portal of the Eisenhower Tunnel.

divide, it is 1,496 feet below the surface. The tunnel is about 50 feet high and 1.7 miles long. Costs for the Eisenhower Tunnel exceeded $116.9 million dollars for the westbound bore and $144.9 million for the eastbound bore.

The tunnel is staffed 24-hours a day, 365 days a year. This staff assures the tunnel's safety by providing tunnel washing and maintenance, traffic management, inspections for over-height and hazardous materials vehicles, emergency response, and snow removal.

The tunnel's safety crews monitor from a control room equipped with 38 color monitors attached to 42 cameras that they can tilt, zoom, and pan left and right. This technology permits the crew to respond quickly to vehicle stalls, accidents, or fire.

Full color cameras and sensors at both tunnel portals watch for oversize trucks and haulers of hazardous materials—these vehicles are generally not allowed to use the tunnel, and must go over Loveland Pass instead. Crews use stoplights and sirens to prevent them from entering the tunnel. When US 6 over Loveland Pass is closed, they stop tunnel traffic on the hour to allow oversize trucks and hazardous materials transporters to proceed through the tunnel.

Power for the tunnel and its control rooms, lights, and ventilation system costs about $1,000,000 a year. The tunnel averages 30,000 vehicles per day, with a high of over 50,000. No traffic-related fatalities have been recorded after thirty years and 200 million vehicles.

On some weekend evenings and afternoons, eastbound demand exceeds the maximum volume of the two lanes. When this happens, the westbound tunnel is coned, and signal lights in the tunnel change to indicate two-way traffic in that bore. This allows traffic in that tunnel to proceed with one lane in each direction, thus providing three eastbound lanes.

Guanella Pass

Otter Mountain
12,766 feet
N
Gray Wolf Mountain
13,602 feet
Mount Spalding
13,842 feet
Mount Evans
(not visible)
14,264 feet
Mount Bierstadt
14,060 feet
The
Sawtooth
E
167°

Accessed via the **Guanella Pass** Scenic and Historic Byway, 11,669-foot Guanella Pass skirts the Mount Evans Wilderness and provides panoramic views highlighted by 14,060-foot Mount Bierstadt. The jagged Sawtooth ridge, which connects Mount Beirstadt to fellow fourteener Mount Evans, is also visible from the pass. The pass divides the Clear Creek Canyon drainage on the north and the South Platte drainage on the south.

Hikes leading to both Mount Bierstadt and Mount Evans begin at the large parking lot atop Guanella Pass. Mount Bierstadt, the

ORIGIN OF NAME	Byron Guanella, who served as county commissioner and road superintendent in Clear Creek County
ELEVATION	11,669 feet
NEARBY CITIES	Grant/Georgetown
POINTS OF INTEREST	Georgetown, Georgetown Loop Railroad, mining ruins, Mount Bierstadt
COUNTY	Clear Creek
HIGHWAY	Guanella Pass Scenic and Historic Byway
MILEPOST	12.9
GPS	39°35'42"N by 105°42'40"W
TOPO MAP	Mount Evans
GETTING THERE	**From Grant** on US 285, travel north on County Road 62. Continue 15 miles. **From Georgetown** on I-70, travel south on County Road 381 for 9 miles.

Scenic Byway

38th highest peak in Colorado, offers one of the easier climbs of a Colorado fourteener. The elevation gain for the hike is 2,796 feet, and it is only 7.1 miles round-trip. The entire hike is above treeline.

The Guanella Pass Scenic and Historic Byway, a 22-mile dirt roadway, provides access to four-wheel drive roads, biking, hiking, climbing, camping, and many other recreational activities. It branches off I-70 in Georgetown and heads south, reaching Guanella Pass at 11 miles, then continues on to the mining town of Grant.

Like many mountain pass roads, this one started out as a wagon road. It connected the gold and silver mining towns of Georgetown and Grant. These towns are within the mineral belt that ran from near the town of Ward to the area around the town of Creede, passing through Georgetown and Leadville on the way.

Landslide Peak

Fourteeners

Colorado has the highest concentration of high peaks of any state in the U.S. Views across the Rockies make one understand the local saying that "if you smashed Colorado out flat it would be bigger than the state of Texas!" The state has over 1,000 summits higher than 10,000 feet, 750 of which are over 13,000 feet, and 54 of which are higher than 14,000 feet. Climbers call this last group the fourteeners. Mt. Elbert, at 14,440 feet, is the highest and Sunshine Peak, at 14,001feet, is the lowest.

Thousands of people a year bag, or summit, a fourteener. Some of these people refer to themselves as "peak baggers." Two thirds of Colorado's fourteeners do not actually require technical climbing, and are more like long, steep hikes. Though these hikes may not require any technical knowledge, they are still dangerous, and proper planning and preparation is a prerequisite for any fourteener attempt.

Rules of Peak Bagging

One "rule" that most peak baggers recognize is that a peak must be at least 300 feet above the saddle that connects it to the nearest peak in order for it to be considered a separate mountain. The number of fourteeners in Colorado is 52 to 59 depending on who makes the list and what "rules" they apply. Most resources place the number at 54, but older copies of the Official Map to Colorado only listed 53. A query of The Geographic Names Information System (GNIS) lists only 48 Colorado peaks as being over 14,000 feet.

An additional rule that some baggers recognize is that you must climb 3,000 vertical feet to reach the summit or the ascent does not count. This rule exists because some peaks, such as Mount Evans

Fourteener Mount Evans and the Sawtooth, which connects it to fourteener Mount Bierstadt.

and Pikes Peak, have roads to their summits. Additionally, traversing up and down ridges to gain a total of 3,000 vertical feet does not count. Based on this rule, climbing Mt. Evans and Mt. Bierstadt from Guanella Pass would not count, since the elevation gain would only be 2,595 feet and 2,391 feet, respectively!

Serious Baggers

Many people have climbed all of Colorado's fourteeners—some have climbed them all multiple times. In 2001, Ted Keizer climbed 55 fourteeners in 10 days, 20 hours, and 26 minutes. For the runners, there is a marathon race up Pikes Peak every year. Some have bagged all the peaks in the winter months. In 1991, Louis Dawson became the first person to ski down all of Colorado's fourteeners.

Study the Peaks and Use Caution

Climbing is a dangerous activity. Conditions vary dramatically according to time of year and even by time of day. Weather can change dramatically and become life threatening in a short period of time. Anyone who attempts the fourteeners should be in good physical condition, have some level of experience, and be properly equipped. Study up before starting your adventure, and be prepared for changing weather. Always let someone who's not climbing with you know what route you're taking and when you expect to return. Every year there are hundreds of search and rescue efforts for people who attempted a fourteener and got lost, injured because they were not in good physical condition, or were unprepared. Keep in mind that some fourteeners are on private land and permission must be obtained to climb them.

The Sawatch Range, including fourteener Mount of the Holy Cross.

Colorado's 54 Fourteeners

The Colorado Department of Transportation's Official Map to Colorado provides the following order and elevation for the state's fourteeners. Different listings may have different elevations that place the peaks in a different order.

Rank	Peak	Elevation (in feet)	Range	Rank	Peak	Elevation (in feet)	Range
1	Mt. Elbert	14,440	Sawatch	28	Mt. Sneffels	14,150	San Juan
2	Mt. Massive	14,421	Sawatch	29	Mt. Democrat	14,148	Tenmile-Mosquito
3	Mt. Harvard	14,420	Sawatch	30	Capitol Peak	14,130	Elk
4	Blanca Peak	14,345	Sangre de Cristo	31	Pikes Peak	14,110	Front Range
5	La Plata Peak	14,336	Sawatch	32	Snowmass Mtn.	14,092	Elk
6	Uncompahgre Peak	14,309	San Juan	33	Mt. Eolus	14,083	San Juan
7	Crestone Peak	14,294	Sangre de Cristo	34	Windom Peak	14,082	San Juan
8	Mt. Lincoln	14,286	Tenmile-Mosquito	35	Challenger Point	14,080	Sangre de Cristo
9	Grays Peak	14,270	Front Range	36	Mt. Columbia	14,073	Sawatch
10	Mt. Antero	14,269	Sawatch	37	Culebra Peak	14,069	Sangre de Cristo
11	Torreys Peak	14,267	Front Range	38	Missouri Mountain	14,067	Sawatch
12	Castle Peak	14,265	Elk	39	Humboldt Peak	14,064	Sangre de Cristo
13	Quandary Peak	14,265	Tenmile-Mosquito	40	Mt. Bierstadt	14,060	Front Range
14	Mt. Evans	14,264	Front Range	41	Sunlight Peak	14,059	San Juan
15	Longs Peak	14,255	Front Range	42	Handies Peak	14,048	San Juan
16	Mt. Wilson	14,246	San Juan	43	Ellingwood Point	14,042	Sangre de Cristo
17	Mt. Shavano	14,229	Sawatch	44	Mt. Lindsey	14,042	Sangre de Cristo
18	Mt. Belford	14,197	Sawatch	45	Little Bear Peak	14,037	Sangre de Cristo
19	Crestone Needle	14,197	Sangre de Cristo	46	Mt. Sherman	14,036	Tenmile-Mosquito
20	Mt. Princeton	14,197	Sawatch	47	Redcloud Peak	14,034	San Juan
21	Mt. Yale	14,196	Sawatch	48	Pyramid Peak	14,018	Elk
22	Mt. Bross	14,172	Tenmile-Mosquito	49	Wilson Peak	14,017	San Juan
23	Kit Carson Peak	14,165	Sangre de Cristo	50	Wetterhorn Peak	14,017	San Juan
24	El Diente Peak	14,159	San Juan	51	San Luis Peak	14,014	San Juan
25	Maroon Peak	14,156	Elk	52	Mt. of the Holy Cross	14,005	Sawatch
26	Tabeguache Peak	14,155	Sawatch	53	Huron Peak	14,005	Sawatch
27	Mt. Oxford	14,153	Sawatch	54	Sunshine Peak	14,001	San Juan

Climbing Colorado's fourteeners does not always require technical equipment, but it does require good sense.

Avoiding the Crowds

It is estimated that there are between 200,000 and 500,000 attempts to climb a fourteener each year. While climbing Grays Peak a few years ago, I passed 25 people headed down who already made the summit, then I ate lunch with 75 on the summit, and passed another 175 people still ascending the peak on my way back down. This was not a guess—I counted them!

Hypothermia is the most common cause of death in the mountains.

It is difficult to think about solitude when experiencing crowds like this. Fortunately, these massive peaks provide many routes for the climber seeking one less traveled. Many of the peaks remain pristine, but the impact of all these climbers has environmentalists very concerned. Numerous organizations now work to preserve the fourteeners and provide ample opportunities for volunteers to contribute to the effort.

Some call the thirty-minute drive near Buena Vista, on one section of US 24, "The Highway of the Fourteeners." From the highway the traveler can see a total of ten 14,000-foot peaks, a truly unique view.

There are a lot of mountains in Colorado and not all of them require the effort of a fourteener. Standing on any peak with the world below creates a memorable and satisfying experience.

Mount Evans

Views from the Mount Evans summit are enormous. On a clear day it is possible to identify peaks 150 miles away.

Torreys Peak
14,267 feet
Mount Bierstadt
14,060 feet
Grays Peak
14,278 feet
The Sawtooth
14,267 feet
Landslide Peak
13,238 feet
Revenue Mountain
12,889 feet
Mount McClellan
13,587 feet
E
89°

The **Mt. Evans** Scenic Byway does not cross a pass, but saying that it is simply a road to the top of a mountain is an understatement! Ending at a parking lot at 14,130 feet, this highway is the highest in North America. A 0.25-mile trail beginning at the parking lot leads hikers to the top of 14,264-foot Mt. Evans. Travelers to Mt. Evans will see panoramic views, alpine tundra, the Meyer-Womble Observatory, and the Mt. Evans Research Station.

*The survey marker on the summit is stamped 14,258 feet, but it is no longer accurate. The U.S. Geological Survey improved cartographic accuracy in 2002 and re-set the official elevations of many peaks.

ORIGIN OF NAME	John Evans was the governor of the Colorado Territory from 1862 to 1865, and the founder of the University of Denver.
ELEVATION	14,134 feet*
NEARBY CITY	Idaho Springs
POINTS OF INTEREST	Mt Evans summit, Summit Lake, Echo Lake
COUNTY	Clear Creek
HIGHWAY	CO 5/Mount Evans Scenic Byway
MILEPOST	16
GPS	39°35'19"N by 105°38'36"W
TOPO MAP	Mount Evans
GETTING THERE	**From Idaho Springs** on I-70, take exit 240. Follow CO 103 south for 15 miles to the Mount Evans Entrance Station. Continue south on CO 5 for 15 miles to the summit of Mount Evans. Road closed in winter.

Scenic Byway

Looking out towards Colorado's eastern plains.

Tundra located off the Mount Evans Highway.

Mount Evans Wilderness Area

The Mt. Evans Wilderness Area, designated by Congress in 1980, is located within the Arapaho and Pike National Forests. A non-wilderness corridor is designated through its center to allow the Mt. Evans Scenic Byway. Most of the 74,300-acre wilderness area, which includes Mt. Evans and Mt. Bierstadt, can be viewed from the summit of Mt. Evans. Half of the wilderness area is above treeline.

Wilderness Area

"An area where the Earth and its communities of life are untrammeled by man, where man himself is just a visitor."

—United States Congress

Today, the Colorado Department of Transportation (CDOT) maintains the road to Mt. Evans, and Denver Mountain Parks administers the areas surrounding Summit Lake, Echo Lake, and Echo Lake Lodge. The South Platte Ranger District of the Pike National Forest and the Clear Creek Ranger District of the Arapaho National Forest control access to and manage the Mount Evans Wilderness Area. For more information, visit wilderness.net.

A billy goat relaxing on the tundra.

Chicago Lake and the Mount Evans Wilderness Area.

High Altitude Astronomical Observatory

The Department of Physics and Astronomy at the University of Denver (DU) manages the 14,148-foot Mt. Evans Meyer-Womble Observatory, the highest operating astronomical observatory in the West. The university completed the building in 1996 and installed the telescope that fall. A radio link from the DU campus 35 miles away allows the telescope to be operated remotely.

Mt. Evans' high elevation and accessibility make it ideal for a telescope. Telescopes that are on high peaks get a clearer view of the universe since they do not have to penetrate as much pollution and water vapor as telescopes at lower elevations.

Until 2001, the Meyer-Womble Observatory was the world's highest astronomical observatory. However, India now runs an observatory and telescope atop 14,763-foot Mt. Saraswati.

Brutal Weather

The Mt. Evans Research Station, the second-highest manned weather station in the country, is also situated on the summit. This location has recorded winds up to 224 miles per hour, snowfall of 500 inches, and a wind-chill temperature of -198° F.

Mount Rosalie

In 1863, Albert Bierstadt, a famous American painter, named a towering mountain Mt. Rosalie, after his wife. In 1870, however, that mountain was renamed Mt. Evans after John Evans, the second governor of the Colorado Territory and founder of the University of Denver. Evans had a great interest in mapping and surveying the Colorado Territory.

As you ascend the peak, the temperature drops according to the adiabatic lapse rate—that is, it drops 5° F for every 1000 feet of elevation gained in a stable air mass. If, on a cool summer morning, temperatures read 60° F at nearby 10,600-foot Echo Lake, it is likely that they will be close to 40° F at Mt. Evans' 14,264-foot summit. Add in the wind chill factor for a 30 mph wind, and it feels like 28° F, making it hard to imagine it is still summer!

Weather conditions change dramatically and quickly at high elevations. Be cautious and pay close attention to weather, especially if you decide to take a walk or a hike. Snowstorms are possible on any day of the year. Sunlight is 40 percent stronger. There is 40 percent less oxygen than at sea level. The relative humidity might be as low as 15 percent. Lightning storms also pose intermittent dangers, so stay away from exposed areas and get to a lower elevation if you see storm clouds developing.

Colorado averages more lightening injuries and fatalities a year than any other state.

A Road to the Top of a Mountain

In 1888, The Cascade and Pikes Peak Toll Road Company, near Colorado Springs, built a 16-mile road to the summit of 14,110-foot Pikes Peak. Denver Mayor Robert W. Speer believed that the Pikes Peak road drew tourists away from Denver, so in 1910 he proposed a road to the top of Mt. Evans, only 35 miles directly west of his city.

In 1917, Speer obtained state funds to build the road. It was completed in 1927. Originally destined to be part of a "Peak-to-Peak Highway" that would travel from the Longs Peak area to Pikes Peak, the road to Mt. Evans ended at 14 miles and never made it any further.

Top: Summit Lake, designated a National Historic Landmark, is located off the Mount Evans Highway. Left: Parking lot at the summit of Mount Evans. Behind what remains of the Crest House is the Denver University Observatory. The dome-shaped buildings contain telescopes.

In the summer of 1942, the Denver Mountain Parks completed Crest House, a summit house atop Mt. Evans. At the time it was the highest structure in the world. The star-shaped structure with arching walls contained a restaurant and a gift and souvenir shop. The fresh donuts made at Crest House were a hit with the tourists, who enjoyed them along with the spectacular views of Denver and the Front Range.

The Mount Evans Highway winds its way around Rogers Peak and Mount Warren.

On September 1, 1979, a propane explosion burned the wood in the structure, leaving a skeleton of stone walls. The Crest House was not rebuilt, but U.S. Forest Service workers responsible for Arapaho National Forest stabilized the walls in 1992 to create a viewing platform.

The Oldest Pines

A drive to the top of Mt. Evans requires a climb of almost 4,000 feet and takes the driver past treeline and onto alpine tundra. A stop at treeline on the way to the top provides an opportunity to examine an extraordinary tree: the ancient bristlecone pine. Trees at treeline have to withstand incredible weather extremes, including freezing cold temperatures, strong winds, and intense solar radiation that would kill most plants. The bristlecone pine has many special adaptations that allow it to survive here.

Bristlecone pines survive because they do not grow like other pine trees. Their branches are more flexible than most pines so they do not break in strong winds. Their wood is very dense, which prevents disease and insects from penetrating it—the dry air and cold temperatures at this elevation also reduce disease-causing bacteria and rot-promoting fungi. The needles on many species of pines are replaced every few years, but to save energy, bristlecones may take as many as 20 to 30 years to replace all their needles. Bristlecone pines often show large areas of dead wood—some have only a thin strip of living bark. The trees growing in the most extreme conditions, with little moisture or soil, often survive the longest.

The largest living bristlecone pine, the Patriarch, boasts a girth of 37 feet.

The trees growing on Mt. Evans may be some of the oldest living trees in the state. Thousand-year-old trees are not uncommon on this mountain, but a bristlecone pine in California currently stands as the Earth's oldest living single organism. The tree, named "Methuselah," is nearly 4,800 years old—a thousand years older than any other known tree.

Bristlecones often grow in protected areas behind rocks or ridges.

Mature bristlecone pine krummholz.

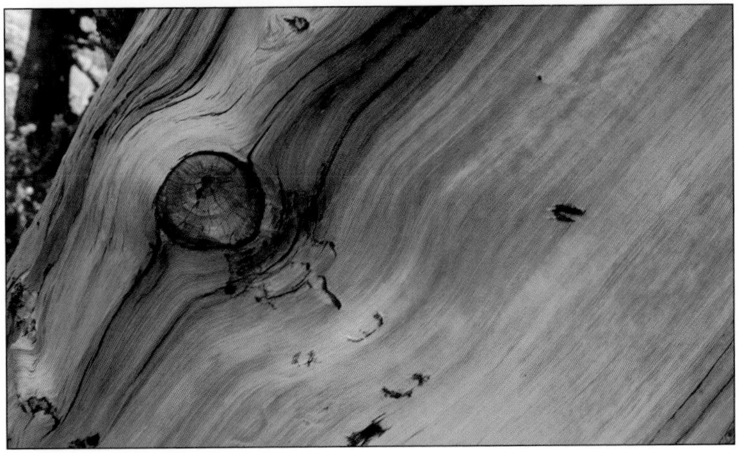

Left: Bristlecone pines have strong, dense wood. Windblown ice and grit polish the outer layers. Above: A bristlecone pine grows close to the ground and away from prevailing winds.

Since the growing season at this elevation is only about 45 days, these trees don't waste their energy by growing fast. A 6-foot-tall tree may be hundreds of years old. Even very old trees growing in protected areas may be only 15 feet tall. In Colorado, bristlecone pines are more common in the southern Rockies; Mt. Evans defines the northernmost extent of their range.

This tree's scientific name is *Pinus aristata*. Arista, meaning "beard," refers to the bristles on their cones.

Vail Pass

Copper Mountain Ski Area and the Ten Mile Range viewed from near Vail Pass.

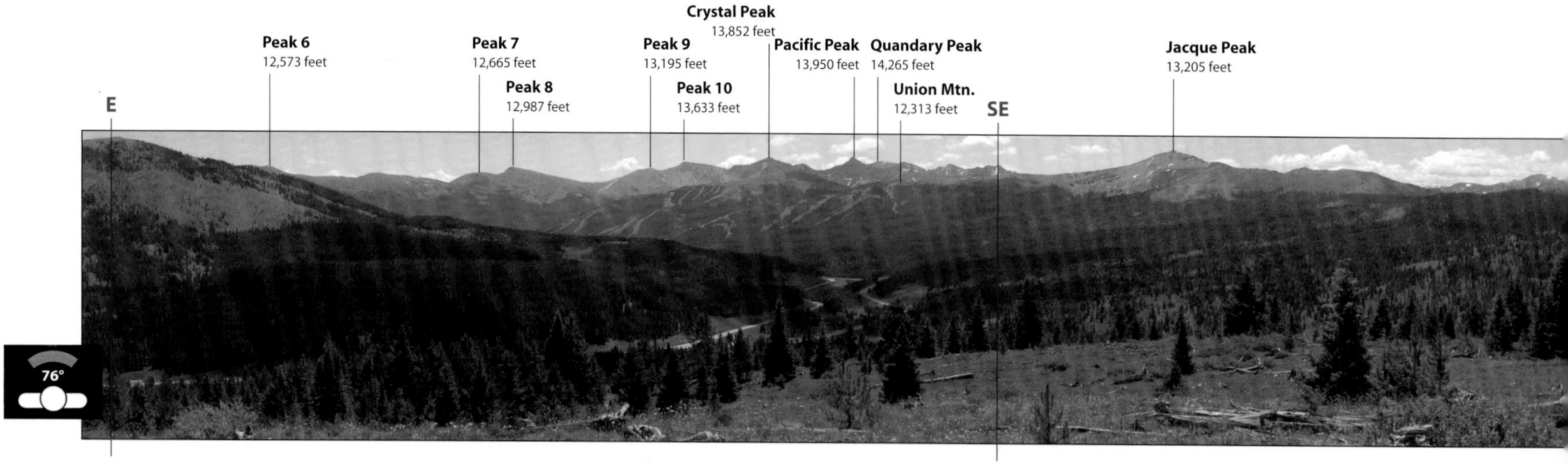
Crystal Peak
13,852 feet
Peak 6
12,573 feet
Peak 7
12,665 feet
Peak 9
13,195 feet
Pacific Peak
13,950 feet
Quandary Peak
14,265 feet
Jacque Peak
13,205 feet
Peak 8
12,987 feet
Peak 10
13,633 feet
Union Mtn.
12,313 feet
E
SE
76°

Vail Pass lies on I-70, 10 miles east of the town of Vail and the famous Vail Mountain Ski Resort. From the top of Vail Pass, a person can see the slopes of Copper Mountain Resort, but not those of Vail. A bike path, which offers a great ride for both the leisurely and serious bicyclist, crosses the pass and connects Copper Mountain and Vail. A large rest area and parking area at the summit offers respite for the car traveler and the bicyclist. Snowmobilers and cross-country skiers also use the pass as a trailhead for winter activities.

ORIGIN OF NAME	Named in 1939 for Charles Vail, chief engineer for the Colorado Highway Department from 1930 to 1945.
ELEVATION	10,666 feet
NEARBY CITIES	Vail/Frisco
POINTS OF INTEREST	Town of Vail, Vail Mountain Ski Resort, Shrine Pass Road, Copper Mountain Ski Area, Gore Range
COUNTY	Summit
HIGHWAY	US 6, I-70
MILEPOST	190
GPS	39°31'50"N by 106°13'02"W
TOPO MAP	Vail Pass
GETTING THERE	**From Vail,** travel east on I-70 for 15 miles to the summit of Vail Pass. **From Frisco,** drive west on I-70 for 12 miles to the summit of Vail Pass.

The Gore Range and Vail ski area viewed from Vail Mountain.

To the west and north of the summit of Vail Pass extends the beautiful Gore Range. Very little of the overall range can be seen from the highway or from the town of Vail. A short trip along the Shrine Pass road provides the most spectacular view of the entire range—take exit 190 off I-70 and go west for 2 miles.

Choosing a Pass

In September 1939, the State Highway Department paved a route over what was then called Black Gore Pass. This was the first highway through the area. At this time, they renamed the pass Vail Pass in honor of Charles Vail, chief engineer for the department.

When they were planning the route, Vail favored a crossing over Red Buffalo Pass, a location north of Vail Pass that would allow the road to be nearly 11 miles shorter. However, Red Buffalo Pass is located in the Gore Range–Eagles Nest Primitive Area of the Arapaho and White River National Forests, and therefore protected from new highway construction. In 1941, Congress did approve reducing the size of the primitive area, established in 1933, to accommodate the construction of US 6 over Vail Pass. In the 1960s, when federal and state highway planners evaluated routes for a new interstate highway system intended to connect major cities of the United States, US 6 over Vail Pass received the nod for the link between Denver and Grand Junction.

Vail—The Ski Area

In the 1950s, Tenth Mountain Division trooper Peter Seibert and Vail rancher Earl Eaton hiked to the top of the mountain that would become the Vail ski area. They knew that the vast open bowls would give the world perfect ski slopes.

In January 1962, the United States Forest Service granted Seibert and Eaton a permit to develop the area. Vail opened in December of that year and grew to become the largest ski area in North America. When Vail first opened, they had one gondola and two chairlifts. Eight ski instructors handled the lessons and a lift ticket cost $5. 2007 statistics are dramatically different:

- Skiable Area: 5,289 acres
- Trails: 193
- Total Lifts: 32
- Lift ticket: $89
- Total Skier/Snowboarder Visits in 2006-2007: 1,608,000
- Total Instructors (full and part time): 800+

The Gore Range, viewed from the Shrine Mountain Trail.

The Gore Range

Sir St. George Gore, the infamous Anglo-Irish baronet, was one of the first white men to pass through this area. Jim Bridger, a famous mountain man, led Gore on a hunting expedition in 1854. Bridger, Gore, and twenty-eight others worked their way to the Colorado River in what is now Grand County near Kremmling. At that time their maps marked the river as the Grand River.

Settlers later put Gore's name on Gore Pass, Gore Canyon near the town of Kremmling, and the Gore Range north of Vail, even though Sir Gore never hunted or traveled in any of these areas. American Indians and white settlers did not like Gore because it was said his party killed two thousand buffalo, sixteen hundred elk and deer, and one hundred bears—an extravagant slaughter.

Some consider the Gore Range to be the most rugged mountain range in Colorado. It is dominated more by dense ridges than high peaks. The separate ridges in the range include: Zodiac Spires, Rockinghorse Ridge, Ripsaw Ridge, and the Grand Traverse. Visitors to the town of Vail can view the Grand Traverse from main street, called Gore Creek Drive. Another beautiful vantage point for the Gore Range, winter or summer, is from the top of virtually any point in the Vail ski area.

The Gore Range is not as popular with climbers and hikers as other ranges in Colorado for many reasons:

- No point in the range exceeds the 14,000-foot mark.
- No mining roads penetrate the range, so most peaks can only be accessed via a very long approach.
- Private property on the east side makes access difficult, and the trails are often poorly defined.

John Wesley Powell, for whom Mount Powell is named, lost most of his arm in the Battle of Shiloh during the Civil War.

In addition, it is difficult to brag about conquering a peak in this range because few of them even have names, and many are difficult to identify on a map. In 1932, the Colorado Mountain Club attempted to address this problem by using letters to mark the summits in one part of the range. Though this lettering system frustrated hikers, it is still used, and has expanded to encompass more peaks in the range.

Some peaks in this range do carry names. They include:

- Bald Mountain
- The Partners (East and West)
- Eagles Nest
- Mount Silverthorne
- East Thorn
- The Spider

The Gore Range actually extends from Rabbit Ears Pass to Fremont Pass. The highest point in the range, visible from the Vail area, is Mount Powell. This peak is among the easiest to climb in this complex range. Mount Powell commemorates the famed one-armed Civil War veteran and explorer Major John Wesley Powell. Powell, best known for his expeditions down the Colorado River of the Grand Canyon, also climbed this peak and many others in the Rockies. He first summited this peak with Ned Farrell in 1868.

The Gore Range lies entirely within the Eagles Nest Wilderness Area, one of Colorado's oldest wilderness areas. The area was originally designated the Gore Range–Eagles Nest Primitive Area in 1932 and included 32,400 acres. The United States Congress designated the Eagles Nest Wilderness in 1976, and it now totals 133,311 acres. The wilderness area ranges in elevation from 7,850 to 13,534 feet and includes 180 miles of trails.

White-tailed jackrabbit.

What's in a Name?

In the late 1800s, the surge in the exploration, mining, and settlement of the West drew attention to the problems of not having a standardized naming process. Some locations accumulated a whole list of different names during their history. The town of Independence, near Aspen, has carried the names Farwell, Sparkill, Mount Hope, Chipeta, and Mammoth City. Bowen Mountain in Rocky Mountain National Park is named for a man named Bourn, but the mapmakers of the time could not read the handwriting on the local maps and put down Bowen.

In 1890 President Benjamin Harrison signed an executive order that established the United States Board on Geographic Names. He gave the board authority to resolve all issues related to geographic names. All entities of the U.S. federal government were required to adhere to its decisions. President Theodore Roosevelt further strengthened the power of the board in 1906. In 1947 Congress reorganized the board to work with the secretary of the interior to establish and maintain uniform geographic name usage throughout the federal government.

Today the board includes representatives of many federal agencies. The board asserts its own principles, policies, and procedures governing the application and use of geographic names. They manage information on more than 2.5 million physical, cultural, and geographic features in the United States and its territories. Their records include the names of natural features, populated places, civil and governmental divisions, areas and regions, and cultural features such as mines, churches, schools, cemeteries, hospitals, dams, airports, and shopping centers.

The Geographic Names Information System (GNIS) is the federal standard for geographic nomenclature, maintained in a database called The National Geographic Names Database. The United States Geological Survey maintains this database. The GNIS website at http://geonames.usgs.gov/pls/gnispublic has a searchable data base that includes almost two million features grouped by many different categories. Each record contains the official or primary name, a term identifying the kind of feature, the location of the feature by state, county, and geographic coordinates, the base series map on which the feature is located, the elevation if appropriate, variant names, and spellings. Still, confusion remains! There are two Mount Evans in Colorado and dozens of Bear Lakes.

One of the board's operating principles for naming features involves the search for present-day local usage. To do this it works with state and local governments as well as the general public. Place names usually originate from or are influenced by common usage and spoken language. Many geographic names are binomial—they have two parts, one is specific and the other is generic, as in Vail Pass. The specific part identifies the particular place, feature, or area, while the generic part usually identifies a single topographic feature such as mountain, river, or pass.

An individual can apply to have a feature added to the database or changed, but the public as a whole has input into the final decision made by the board. An individual cannot simply submit a random name or have a place named after them or a friend. The name must have some significance to the area, have some historical context, and be acceptable to the public. Studying the place names of features near a geographic area reveals much about the history of an area.

Many of Colorado's features carry the names of individuals who were important to its history. Mountains like Pikes Peak, Longs Peak, and Mount Powell, and features like Gore Pass and Estes Park are good examples. Lone Eagle Peak honors Charles Lindbergh.

Named features also honor events, like the unofficial peak that was renamed Columbia Point to honor the crew of the space shuttle Columbia. Columbia Point is located on the east side of Kit Carson Mountain in the Sangre De Cristos. On the northwest shoulder of the same mountain is Challenger Point, a peak named to honor the space shuttle Challenger. Both shuttles were destroyed in accidents that claimed the lives of their entire crews.

Fremont Pass

Looking east from Freemont Pass towards the Climax Molybdenum Mine.

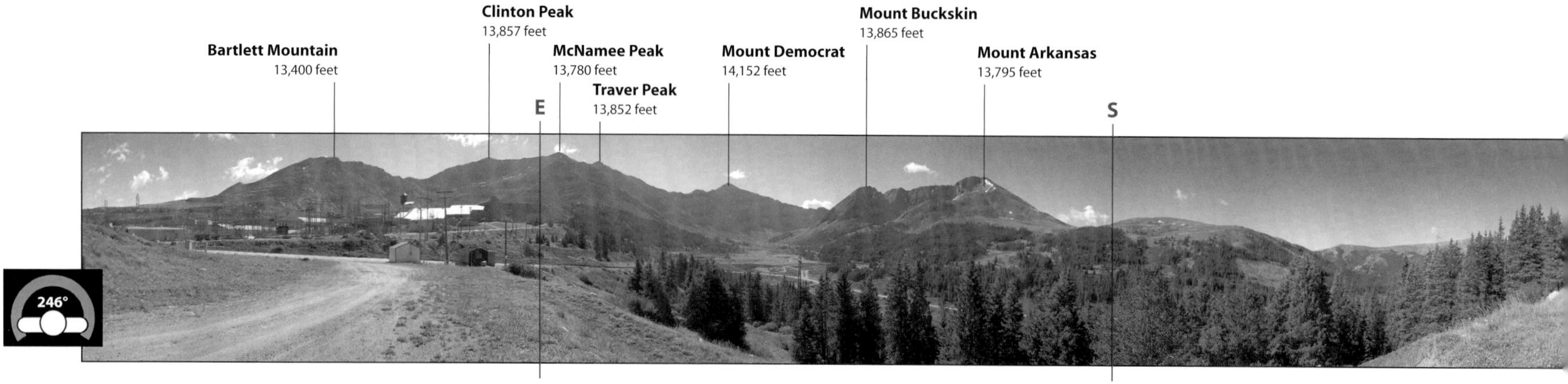
Clinton Peak
13,857 feet
Mount Buckskin
13,865 feet
Bartlett Mountain
13,400 feet
McNamee Peak
13,780 feet
Mount Democrat
14,152 feet
Mount Arkansas
13,795 feet
Traver Peak
13,852 feet
E
S
246°

Human impact is starkly evident on the summit of **Fremont Pass,** located about 11 miles southwest of Frisco on CO 91. Since the late 1870s, miners have worked the area. The Climax Molybdenum Mine located here was once the world's leading producer of molybdenum, accounting for 75 percent of the world's supply. Travelers going over the pass cannot miss how this level of mining activity dramatically changed the scenery here. Below the pass, in the Tenmile Valley, you can see the waste from 400 million tons of molybdenite

ore that have been mined from this area. About 99 percent of the mined material is not used, and it now fills three huge tailings ponds.

Even though the summit of Freemont Pass sits at 11,318 feet—making it the eighth highest pass in Colorado—the approaches from either side are among the most gentle of any pass in the state. The pass sits on the Continental Divide and divides the watershed of the Blue River on the west and the Arkansas River to the east.

At one time, the Denver, South Park and Pacific Railroad and the Colorado and Southern Railway lines crossed Freemont Pass. The remains of their grades can be seen on both approaches to the summit. Today, a railroad tourist line, the Leadville, Colorado & Southern Railroad, originates in Leadville and follows the grade of the defunct railroads to a point near Fremont Pass.

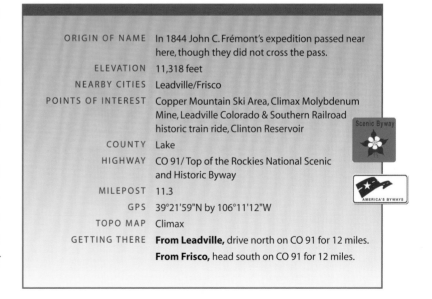

ORIGIN OF NAME	In 1844 John C. Frémont's expedition passed near here, though they did not cross the pass.
ELEVATION	11,318 feet
NEARBY CITIES	Leadville/Frisco
POINTS OF INTEREST	Copper Mountain Ski Area, Climax Molybdenum Mine, Leadville Colorado & Southern Railroad historic train ride, Clinton Reservoir
COUNTY	Lake
HIGHWAY	CO 91/ Top of the Rockies National Scenic and Historic Byway
MILEPOST	11.3
GPS	39°21'59"N by 106°11'12"W
TOPO MAP	Climax
GETTING THERE	**From Leadville,** drive north on CO 91 for 12 miles. **From Frisco,** head south on CO 91 for 12 miles.

Right: Looking west from the summit of Freemont Pass in 2007. Below: The same view, shot by William Henry Jackson in the late 1800s.

Left: Looking south from the summit of Freemont Pass in 2007. Below: The same view, shot by William Henry Jackson in the late 1800s.

The Great Pathfinder

John C. Frémont's second expedition in 1844 is the earliest recorded European exploration in this area. His party visited the region and the sites that are now Dillon, Fremont Pass, the Mosquito Range, the Blue River, Middle Park, and Hoosier Pass. They followed many of the old American Indian trails in the area.

Climax Molybdenum Company

In 1879 Charles Senter staked a gold ore claim on Bartlett Mountain on Fremont Pass. The ore turned out to be molybdenum, and the Climax Molybdenum Company soon formed to mine the metal, which at the time was used in lightbulb filaments.

Molybdenum is an element with a very high melting point, and when added to steel it acts as a hardening agent. World War II increased the demand for this high-strength steel, and a molybdenum-enhanced alloy is still used today. Molybdenum is also heat-resistant and corrosion-resistant, so is often used in aircraft and missiles. It also has uses in petroleum products, lubricants, and electronic parts.

While the mine was in operation, it employed thousands of people, many of whom lived onsite in the town of Climax. Employee housing, a school, and a hospital were once located there. Many of these buildings were later moved to Leadville and are still in use in that town. The Climax Molybdenum Company also developed Chalk Mountain, located west of Red Mountain Pass, as a ski area. They installed a rope tow to service the 1,500-foot slope, and lined the slopes with floodlights, creating Colorado's first night skiing facility.

The morning sun warms the shores of Clinton Reservoir.

CLIMAX MOLYBDENUM COMPANY

The Climax Molybdenum Mine.

Reclamation

Today, the open pit mine on Ceresco Ridge, a dominant feature on Fremont Pass, and the appearance of the mine buildings give the impression that the mine still operates. The mine is not currently operational, however, though there are a handful of full-time employees who care for the facility in the event that it were to reopen. Others work on the environmental reclamation of the area, including restoration of the land, and on water treatment.

The pass averages 23 feet of snow each year, and three major rivers originate near it: the Arkansas, the Eagle, and Tenmile Creek. Many towns rely upon these rivers as a water source, and therefore hold great concern about the water's quality and the treatment it receives. The Climax Molybdenum Company treats the water that comes in contact with the tailings ponds, and wastewater-treatment districts in the area are helping to recover the ponds. The municipal wastewater plants truck their sludge to the Climax ponds, where it

Climax Molybdenum Mine tailing ponds on the north side of the summit. A large environmental cleanup operation is currently underway to restore the valley.

is mixed with wood chips and other bio-solids to create topsoil. Trees and other vegetation are being planted on the site, but at 11,000 feet, where the growing season is only ten weeks, reclamation is a very difficult process.

A major wayside exhibit is planned for the summit of the pass as a feature of the Top of the Rockies Scenic and Historic Byway. The plan includes interpretive panels to explain the mining activity of the area and a display of mining artifacts.

Boreas Pass

Looking toward the Boreas Pass summit.

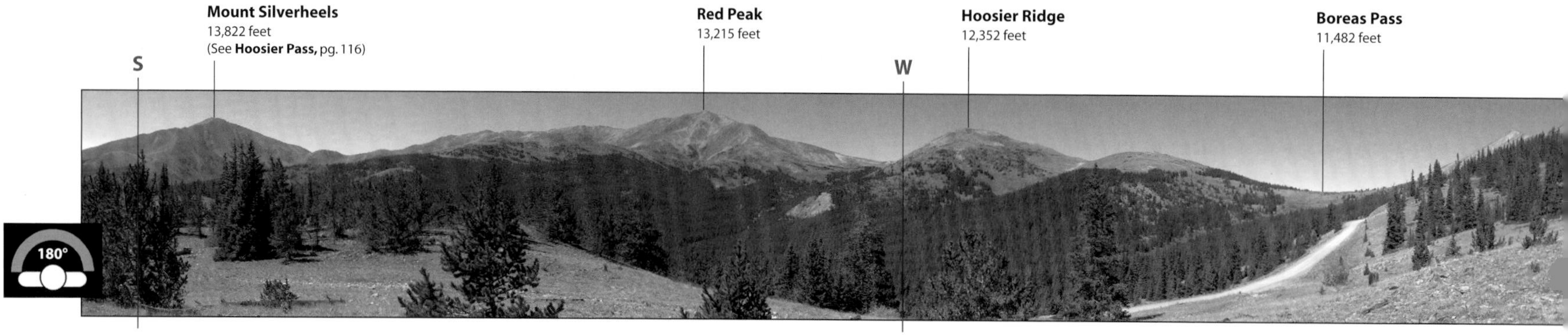
Mount Silverheels
13,822 feet
(See **Hoosier Pass,** pg. 116)
Red Peak
13,215 feet
Hoosier Ridge
12,352 feet
Boreas Pass
11,482 feet
S
W
180°

Boreas, the Greek god of the North Wind, is an appropriate namesake for this pass. Located just below treeline, at an elevation of 11,482 feet, and on the Continental Divide, it endures cold, strong winds, particularly in winter. The pass, originally called Breckenridge Pass, is about 9 miles east of Breckenridge on Boreas Pass Road/Primary Forest Route 10. The well-graded dirt road may be closed during the winter. The pass, which links Breckenridge and Como, remains a popular local drive, particularly in the fall when the aspen are changing.

Boreas Pass was an important stop for the Denver, South Park and Pacific Railroad's "Highline" between Como and Breckenridge;

the railroad's operations there supported a small town. Though the railroad is no longer functioning, an interpretive site is now located at the summit, thanks to the work of the U.S. Forest Service and the Colorado Historical Society in 1993. It includes a railroad section house, a building called Ken's Cabin, and a railroad boxcar. In 1997 the Summit Huts Association began using the section house as a winter ski hut. The rubble of the original stone engine house, destroyed by a fire in 1909, lies on the opposite side of the road.

The Town of Boreas

In the late 1800s, railroad and construction crews occupied the settlement at the summit, but it also served as a stop for travelers. A section house, engine house, snow sheds, and other buildings on site

ORIGIN OF NAME	The Greek god of the North Wind was named Boreas.
ELEVATION	11,482 feet
NEARBY CITIES	Breckenridge/Fairplay
POINTS OF INTEREST	Breckenridge Ski Resort
COUNTY	Summit
HIGHWAY	Forest Route 10, Forest Route 33
MILEPOST	10.8
GPS	39°24'40"N by 105°58'10"W
TOPO MAP	Topo Map: Boreas Pass
GETTING THERE	**From Breckenridge,** travel east on Boreas Pass Road/Forest Route 10, for 9 miles. **From Fairplay,** travel north on US 285 for 10 miles to Como. Turn west on the Boreas Pass Road/Forest Route 33 and continue 8 miles.

Scenic Byway

Boreas Pass section house.

Stumps remaining from timber cut to build railroad ties, snow sheds, snow fences, and the buildings at Boreas Pass.

supported a permanent population of 150. In 1896, Boreas Pass boasted of having the highest post office in the United States—it operated from January 2, 1896, until January 31, 1906.

Ken's Cabin

Ken's Cabin, built in the 1860s, predates the railroad. It was once called the Wagon Cabin because of its location on the original wagon road. Built over the pass in 1860, this road carried supplies over the divide until rail service between Como and Breckenridge began in 1882. The Wagon Cabin's current name honor's Ken Graff, a local doctor who died in an avalanche in 1955. Even though it is one of the oldest buildings around Breckenridge, it sees continual use as a winter ski hut. Many people enjoy this cozy hut, which contains a kitchen, dining area, and sleeping area.

Boreas Pass Road on a brilliant September day.

Playing Fair

In 1859, a number of prospectors found gold in Tarryall Creek at the base of the east side of what became Boreas Pass. They registered many foot claims along the creek where they panned for gold. Foot claims are sections of a river from 200 to 500 feet in length where a miner would use panning or other placer processes to recover gold. Hundreds of other prospectors soon joined them—eventually, the entire creek was claimed.

The original prospectors refused to divide their claims, even though they were unable to work all the land that they had staked. Latecomers did not find a welcome on the creek, so they moved on south to a place where Beaver Creek joins the Middle Fork of the South Platte River. They called their panning area "Fair Play" because they had received such poor treatment from the prospectors at the Tarryall Diggings. The name stuck, and the current town's name remains Fairplay.

Como and the Como Roundhouse

The town of Como, on US 285 at the base of the east side of Boreas Pass, owes its existence to the Denver, South Park and Pacific Railroad and the local mines. Today, most of its buildings are abandoned, but in the late 1800s the community held 500 to 1000 people.

In the summer of 1879, Como included nearly a dozen wooden buildings. If this town resembled other fast-growing mining and railroad towns, tents dotted the area as well. The town became an important stopping place for train crews as they traveled between Denver, Breckenridge, and Leadville. The railroad constructed a depot, machine shop, blacksmith's shop, and numerous storage buildings. Some still stand today.

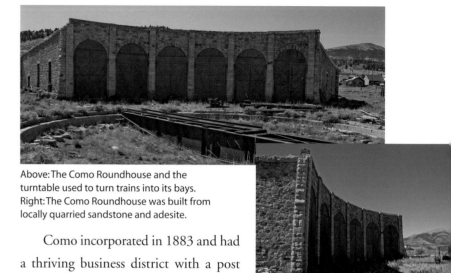

Above: The Como Roundhouse and the turntable used to turn trains into its bays. Right: The Como Roundhouse was built from locally quarried sandstone and adesite.

Como incorporated in 1883 and had a thriving business district with a post office, general store, bakeries, saloons, laundries, barbershops, churches, hotels, and lodges. Como's post office has operated continuously since 1879. As with many mining and railroad towns, the population declined quickly as mining declined. In 1937 its last scheduled passenger train departed for Denver, ending the era of the narrow gauge in South Park.

The most impressive building remaining in Como is the stone roundhouse, built of locally quarried stone in 1881. A roundhouse consists of a round or semi-circular building assembled around a turntable of railroad track. In the simplest of terms, it serves as a garage for trains. Roundhouses have bays to house and service locomotives.

A locomotive entered the roundhouse yard on a single set of tracks connected to a large turntable. The turntable then rotated to allow the train to move down a different set of tracks and into an open bay for maintenance and repairs. The turntable eliminated the need to have a large rail yard and huge amounts of additional track.

The South Park Line

The South Park Line originated in Denver and traveled up the South Platte River valley over Kenosha Pass. It continued as the Denver, South Park and Pacific Railway over Boreas Pass, through Breckenridge, and on into Dillon. The line then turned west and headed up Ten Mile Creek to Wheeler, where Copper Mountain Ski Area is now located. It turned south at Wheeler and traveled through the towns of Kokomo and Climax before crossing over Fremont Pass and into Leadville. The line actually crossed the Continental Divide twice, once at Boreas Pass and again at Fremont Pass. This line was one of three railroads that eventually reached Leadville.

At the time of its completion, the Alpine Tunnel along the South Park Line was the highest and most expensive tunnel ever built.

The Denver, South Park and Pacific Railway became the Denver, Leadville and Gunnison Railroad in 1889. That line merged with other lines in the same year to become the Colorado and Southern Railroad. Overall, the line operated from 1873 to 1937. The Army Corp of Engineers removed the tracks and the railroad bed in 1938. An automobile road replaced the railroad bed in 1956.

Left: Short section of restored track east of the Boreas Pass summit. Below: View looking east over South Park from the Davis Overlook at Boreas Pass.

View looking north toward Breckenridge from 1 mile west of Boreas Pass.

At one time thirteen wooden bays extended from the original six-bay stone roundhouse at Como. However, mining activity in the area began to decrease in the early 1900s; and the Alpine Tunnel, by which the line connected to Gunnison and the western slope, collapsed in 1910. Both of these factors significantly and adversely affected the economic fortune of the line. Most of the wooden bays were demolished around 1918, and in 1935 the heat of a locomotive set fire to a bird nest in the building and burned down the remaining three wooden bays. Only the original stone structure remains today.

Disastrous fires were common events in the late 1800s and early 1900s. The heat of the trains and the embers they belched set fire to depots, snowsheds, roundhouses, and forests. Oil lamps, candles, wood fireplaces, and coal stoves caused fires in houses, hotels, and other buildings. Most communities did not have much in the way of fire suppression equipment, so when something did go up in flames, most people could only watch and could do little to stop it.

After the Denver, South Park and Pacific Railway bankruptcy and the removal of the tracks, the Como roundhouse served as a barn, a sawmill, and then a warehouse before being listed as a national historic site in 1983. Over the years some individuals dedicated to restoring the roundhouse have replaced the roof, rebuilt stone walls, and reconstructed the replica doors. The turntable now at the site may indeed be the 1881 original.

Of the large number of roundhouses that once existed across the state, almost all have been torn down. In addition to the one at Como, only two others remain: The Colorado Midland Railroad roundhouse west of Colorado Springs, constructed in 1889, now houses the Van Briggle Art Pottery Company; and the Durango & Silverton Narrow Gauge Railroad maintains the only roundhouse still in use in Colorado—it comprises ten bays and was built in 1881. Located in the town of Durango, it is used to maintain the engines of the Durango & Silverton Narrow Gauge Railroad.

Railroad Rolling Stock

The equipment used on the railroads often changed purpose and to suit its different locations. The boxcar located at the interpretive station at the summit of the pass serves as an excellent example. The Colorado Southern Railway boxcar was built it in 1910 for use on the Leadville-Climax line. During World War II, the United States Army requisitioned it, converting it to a flatcar. After the war, it went to Alaska where it served as a gondola on the White Pass and Yukon Railway. In 1955, it became an idler car (a flatcar used as a spacer between cars that carry very long objects) before being retired from service in 1970. It then moved to Loveland, Colorado, for use on a tourist line. In 1996, it reappeared as a boxcar for the Georgetown Loop. The forest service purchased the car in 2000 and moved it to its current location on Boreas Pass, where it serves as an interpretive display. Is there really anything left of the original boxcar?

The brakeman on a train was sometimes referred to as the "Baby Lifter."

C.&S.
8311
This Colorado and Southern Railway boxcar on display at the summit of Boreas Pass has served many uses.

111
KEEP OFF
This engine, which is on display in Breckenridge, was built by the Baldwin Locomotive Works in Philadelphia in 1926 and used in Central America to haul bananas. It was later purchased by the town of Breckenridge, and is similar to those that were used locally from the late 1800s to the early 1900s.

Hoosier Pass

View from a ridge 0.5 mile west of Hoosier Pass. This view, along with the panorama on the next page, completes a 360-degree spread.

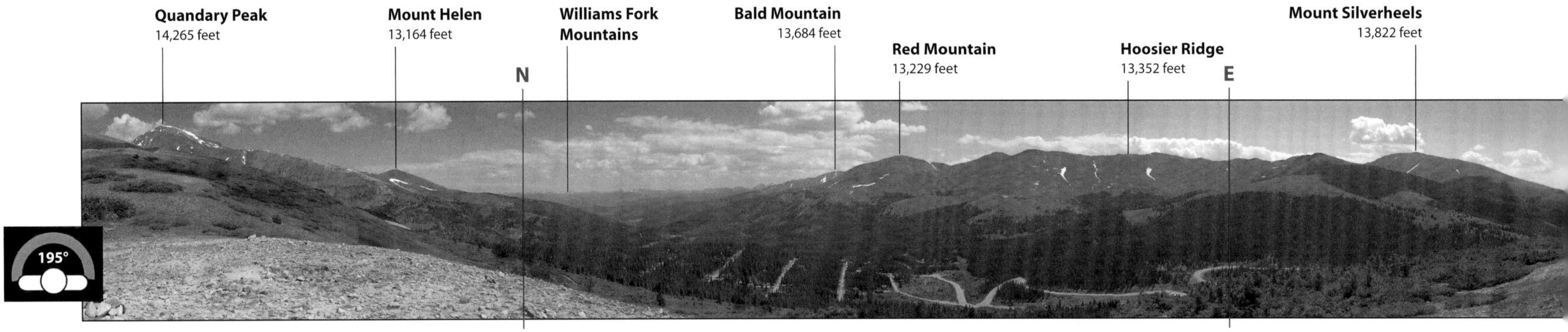
Quandary Peak
14,265 feet
Mount Helen
13,164 feet
N
Williams Fork
Mountains
Bald Mountain
13,684 feet
Red Mountain
13,229 feet
Hoosier Ridge
13,352 feet
E
Mount Silverheels
13,822 feet
195°

The summit of **Hoosier Pass** is 10 miles south of Breckenridge on CO 9. The best views in the area are just a short hike or drive along a 4-wheel-drive road that heads west from the pass. After traveling about a mile, you will find a 360-degree view that includes three fourteeners.

You can still see the remains of what was once a ski area on Hoosier Pass. The area opened in 1938 with two runs, one rope tow, and a warming hut. In later years, several cabins were added, as well as a large restaurant that featured a bar, dancing area, and rest rooms. The business shut down when the rope tow broke in 1949.

Before Colorado was settled, Ute Indians traveled Hoosier Pass to move between their hunting grounds in South Park and Middle Park. The Spaniards entered the area in the 1600s, and on June 23, 1844, American explorer John C. Frémont crossed over Hoosier Pass.

The Story Behind the Name

Dyer Peak

This nearby peak is named for Father John Lewis Dyer, an itinerant Methodist minister who founded a Methodist church in Breckenridge in 1879. Its congregation remains active today in its original structure. Since his ministry did not cover his expenses, Dyer would prospect for gold. Father Dyer loved mountain life, and is best known for his ability to deliver not only the Gospel, but sacks of

ORIGIN OF NAME	Indiana miners named the pass Hoosier, a word that identifies a resident or native of the state of Indiana.
ELEVATION	11,541 feet
NEARBY CITIES	Fairplay/Breckenridge
POINTS OF INTEREST	Breckenridge Ski Resort, mining ruins
COUNTY	Summit
HIGHWAY	CO 9
MILEPOST	76.5
GPS	39°21'42"N by 106°03'45"W
TOPO MAP	Alma
GETTING THERE	**From Fairplay,** travel north on CO 9 for 12 miles to the summit of Hoosier Pass. **From Frisco** on I-70 at exit 203, head south on CO 9 for 11 miles to Breckenridge. Continue on CO 9 for 11 miles to the summit of Hoosier Pass.

Windy Ridge Bristlecone Pine Scenic Area
Middle Fork of the South Platte
S
Mount Bross 14,172 feet
McNamee Peak 13,790 feet
Traver Peak 13,852 feet
Clinton Peak 13,857 feet
North Star Mountain 13,614 feet
153°

gold and mail as well during his travels. He braved deep snow and fierce winter storms on 12-foot wooden skis to deliver the word of God to the scattered towns of the Leadville mining district. In 1863 he signed on to carry the United States mail and nearly died that year in an avalanche. Dyer captured his poignant stories in a book titled *The Snow-Shoe Itinerant*, in which he describes his experiences and solo trips on the high peaks and passes in the area.

Mount Silverheels

Another peak near Hoosier commemorates a woman who, in the winter of 1861, nursed the sick during a deadly small pox epidemic in the town of Buckskin Joe. She became a legend, and Mount Silverheels inherited her name.

Silver Heels was a dance hall girl. In 1861 she arrived in the town of Buckskin Joe, near the present town of Alma, south of Hoosier Pass. Her performances enchanted the miners and, even though she planned to spend only a few days in the town, they convinced her to stay.

Not long after, small pox, which could not be controlled at the time, swept through the mining camp. Many of the miners and their families became very sick and within days many died. They had no access to outside medical help, and those who did not become sick became nurses for those who were. Silver Heels worked tirelessly nursing the sick, caring for their families, and burying the dead.

By spring of 1862 the epidemic subsided, and shortly thereafter, Silver Heels disappeared. The miners and the community searched for her with no success. They knew that she had not left by horse or by stage. A few years later, someone saw a veiled woman in the Buckskin Joe cemetery and reported that she bore a resemblance to Silver Heels. Others also reported apparitions of a veiled woman dressed in black and carrying flowers. All attested that she would vanish when approached.

All that remains of the two runs that once made up the Hoosier Pass Ski Area.

Tailings from a dredging operation west of Fairplay. Right: The South Platte Dredge near Fairplay. Note the tailings piles behind the dredge.

Breckenridge

General George E. Spencer founded the town of Breckenridge in November 1859 and named it after President James Buchanan's vice president, John Cabell Breckinridge. Why is the name of the town spelled differently? At the onset of the Civil War, John Breckinridge received a commission as a brigadier general in the Confederate

Army. That prompted the U.S. Senate to expel Breckinridge for treason. The actions of Breckinridge embarrassed the residents of the town so much that they switched the "i" for an "e." The town has retained its new spelling ever since.

Skiing Saves the Day

In 1960 Breckenridge claimed a population of only 393. Residents feared that it might soon become a ghost town. Then, in 1961, the Rounds and Porter Lumber Company of Wichita, Kansas, obtained a permit to develop a new ski area in Breckenridge. The Breckenridge Ski Resort officially opened in December of 1961 with one double chairlift and a T-bar. Nearly 17,000 skiers visited the area that first season.

Ten years later, in 1971, Peak 9 opened with two double chairs and twelve trails. Skier visits climbed to 221,000 a year. Ten more years passed, and in 1981 Breckenridge installed the world's first high-speed quad chairlift, kicking off the industry's high-speed lift craze. The area's popularity continued to increase, and today Breckenridge records 1.5 million skier visits per season. The white gold of snow turned the Breckenridge economy around when pure gold would no longer support the town.

Dredges

From the early 1920s into the late 1940s, gold miners used dredges to mechanically sift through gravel and silt in search of gold. The huge machines were built on top of gravel deposits surrounded by dams to create a basin. Once the basin was filled, the dredge would float. Long arms fitted with many buckets extend from the machine, digging down as far as 70 feet below water level. A floating dredge could move forward easily into the space it had just excavated, sometimes traveling as far as 200 feet in a day. The excavated material was washed in sluices; gold, being heavier, settled to the bottom of them, and unwanted materials were carried out of the dredge on conveyor belts and deposited in its wake.

Though there is only one remaining dredge in Colorado—The Snowstorm Gold Dredge, located 2 miles north of Fairplay—you can still see evidence of dredging on both sides of Hoosier Pass and elsewhere in the state. Large piles of rock and gravel tailings mark the spots where the dredges unloaded unwanted materials. Dredges unearthed huge amounts of gold, but they destroyed the rivers, valleys, and wetlands around them, and little can be done to recover the extensive areas of sterile tailings they left behind.

Tom's Baby

Breckenridge can lay claim to the largest gold nugget ever found in Colorado. On July 3, 1887, Tom Groves walked into the town carrying something cradled in his arms and wrapped in a blanket. This single golden nugget, weighing 13.5 pounds, became known as "Tom's Baby." Strangely, it disappeared for many years, only to be found in a Denver bank in 1926—five pounds lighter! Tom's Baby is now on display at the Denver Museum of Nature & Science.

Above: Ditches were dug to divert water from nearby creeks and streams into the pond that kept the Snowstorm Gold Dredge floating. Top Right: This large water pipe was used to transport water into the Snowstorm Gold Dredge pond. Right: The Snowstorm Gold Dredge, Colorado's only remaining dredge, located between Fairplay and Alma.

Kenosha Pass

Kenosha Pass. The railroad tracks in the foreground were rebuilt as part of a Denver, South Park and Pacific Railroad interpretive site.

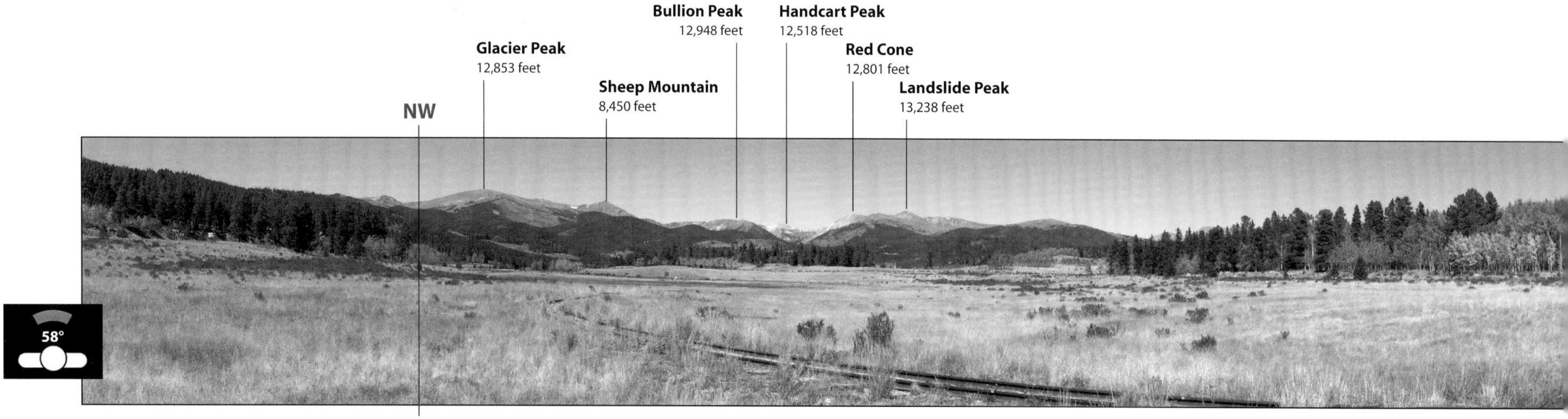
Bullion Peak
12,948 feet
Handcart Peak
12,518 feet
Glacier Peak
12,853 feet
Red Cone
12,801 feet
Sheep Mountain
8,450 feet
Landslide Peak
13,238 feet
NW
58°

Even though 10,000-foot **Kenosha Pass** on the north side of South Park doesn't offer much in the way of scenic views, there are exceptional viewpoints nearby. Views from the meadow just north of the pass are spectacular. The view from a parking lot 0.25 mile south of the pass stretches for more than 50 miles and probably inspires travelers as much today as it did in the late 1800s.

Located 20 miles north of Fairplay on US 285, the pass is between the towns of Jefferson and Grant. The Colorado Trail crosses the highway here. Additionally, the forest service has re-layed a section of the Denver, South Park and Pacific Railroad track and wye in the meadow near the Kenosha Campground and Picnic Area.

ORIGIN OF NAME	A stage driver from Kenosha, Wisconsin, may have named this pass.
ELEVATION	10,001 feet
NEARBY CITIES	Fairplay/Grant
POINT OF INTEREST	South Park
COUNTY	Park
HIGHWAY	US 285
MILEPOST	203.3
GPS	39°24'48"N by 105°45'24"W
TOPO MAP	Jefferson
GETTING THERE	**From Fairplay,** head north on US 285 for 21 miles. **From Grant**, travel south on US 285 for 8 miles.

The Colorado Trail

South Park as seen from Kenosha Pass. The town of Jefferson is on the far left.

Little Baldy
12,142 feet
Mount Silverheels
13,822 feet
Boreas Mountain
13,082 feet
Bald Mountain
13,684 feet
Mount Guyot
13,370 feet
W
86°

An interpretive center discusses the history of this railroad line, which once crossed Kenosha Pass. When you are heading east from the pass, a great deal of the abandoned railroad grade is visible above the highway on the left (north) side of the road.

South Park

The name "South Park" is most frequently associated with the animated television comedy series about four third- and fourth-grade boys who live in the fictional town of South Park, Colorado. There

is also a South Park City, located in the town of Fairplay, Colorado, that is an outdoor living-history museum. The South Park referred to in this book is neither the fictional town nor the museum. It is a high grassland basin located in central Colorado.

The term "park," as it applies to the high country of Colorado, refers to a large open valley surrounded by mountains. Native Americans were the first people to explore South Park. In 1806, American soldier and explorer Zebulon Pike entered the south edge of South Park, and the reports of his explorations drew the attention of hunters and trappers. John C. Fremont's party also passed through the area in 1844.

A railroad frog, or switch, on the Kenosha Pass wye, which allows a train to be sent down either of two sets of tracks.

Zebulon Pike, who explored this area, never summited the mountain that bears his name.

Miners discovered gold near Kenosha pass in 1859, and a wagon road was built over the pass soon after. Lured by the profits of the mines and the prospect of extending their line to California, the Denver, South Park and Pacific Railroad reached Kenosha Pass in1879. A town named Kenosha thrived briefly atop the pass, serving as a convenient stopping place for the trains. From Kenosha, the line continued on to Como, then to the profitable mining towns of Fairplay, Gunnison, Breckenridge, Frisco, and Leadville. The Denver, South Park and Pacific Railroad

Mason Bogie 48 at Alma, Colorado, in 1886.

could not compete with the Denver & Rio Grande Western, however, and eventually fell into bankruptcy. The tracks for the railroad were removed in 1937, and now no railroads traverse South Park.

The Mason Bogie

The Denver, South Park and Pacific Railroad used a special locomotive, called the Mason Bogie, to cope with the steep grade and tight turns that their lines through the Rockies presented. The Mason Bogie was an articulated or "flexible" locomotive; its frame pivoted to provide greater power for the sharp curves and uneven track found on narrow gauge lines such as the one that crossed Kenosha Pass.

Beehive-shaped charcoal kilns at the town of Webster, east of Kenosha Pass.

Bison

Thousands of bison once grazed South Park. The area was an important hunting ground for the Ute. When white settlers came into the West, they almost hunted the bison to extinction. In 1897, hunters in Lost Park—an isolated valley in South Park's northeast corner—shot Colorado's last four bison.

Local ranchers have reintroduced the plains bison. You may see them grazing along Colorado roadsides. Many area restaurants offer buffalo burgers and steaks. Bison meat contains 2 grams of fat per 100 grams of cooked lean meat, compared to 9 grams for beef. Because of its low fat content, bison cooks faster than beef.

Charcoal Production

Companies producing charcoal sprang up throughout the South Park area in the 1880s. Charcoal is created by cooking wood in an oxygen-deprived environment. These companies employed over 300 people in chopping down trees and tending the kilns where the wood was cooked. They produced tons of charcoal and, in the process, decimated nearly all the trees on and around Kenosha pass. The trees seen today have grown back since the kilns shut down in 1893.

Red Hill Pass

View of the Mosquito Range from Red Hill Pass.

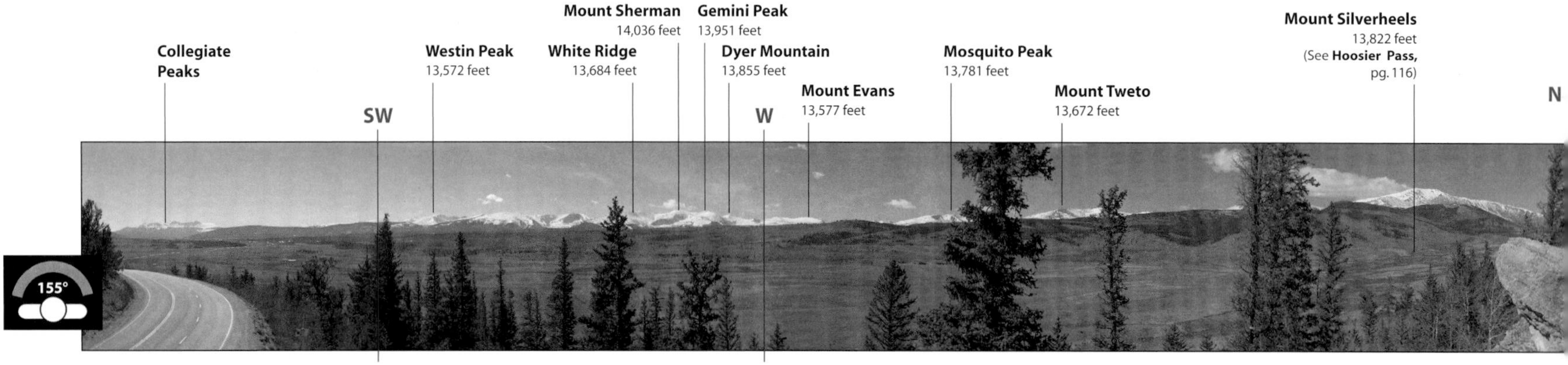
Collegiate Peaks
SW
Westin Peak
13,572 feet
Mount Sherman
14,036 feet
White Ridge
13,684 feet
Gemini Peak
13,951 feet
Dyer Mountain
13,855 feet
W
Mount Evans
13,577 feet
Mosquito Peak
13,781 feet
Mount Tweto
13,672 feet
Mount Silverheels
13,822 feet
(See **Hoosier Pass**, pg. 116)
N
155°

From the top of **Red Hill Pass,** you can look west for a spectacular view of the Mosquito Range. Located on US 285 between Grant and Fairplay, this pass is named for the red sandstone that it cuts through. This rock has been quarried to provide building materials for many structures in Fairplay, about 6 miles southwest of the pass.

Red Hill Pass is located on the railroad grade of the Denver, South Park and Pacific Railroad. As you look down from the pass into the large open valley of South Park, you can make out the railroad grades on the valley floor. The dirt roads across the valley follow those grades in some areas. You can almost imagine what it was like to look out over this valley in the early 1900s, when the only signs of human encroachment were the railroad tracks and the occasional plumes of smoke from the locomotives.

ORIGIN OF NAME	The pass cuts through red sandstone on the top of the ridge. Could also be named for a red-colored mountain not far from the pass.
ELEVATION	9,993 feet
NEARBY CITIES	Fairplay/Grant
POINTS OF INTEREST	Mosquito Range, Fairplay Burro Monuments
COUNTY	Park
HIGHWAY	US 285
MILEPOST	186.5
GPS	39°16'04"N by 105°57'40"W
TOPO MAP	Topo Map: Como
GETTING THERE	**From Fairplay,** travel north on US 285 for 5 miles.
	From Grant, drive south on US 285 for 24 miles.

Burros

For nineteenth century miners, a burro provided important labor as well as companionship. Miners working in the rugged high country of the Colorado Rockies especially valued these small, strong, sure-footed animals. Burros were responsible for carrying millions of dollars worth of ore and supplies along rough, narrow mountain trails. Because of their emotional and material value to the miners, the burros became the subject of songs and legends.

Two monuments in the town of Fairplay honor these animals. One monument, located on Front Street, honors a burro named Prunes who worked in the mines around Fairplay. When Prunes died in 1930, at the age of 63, his owner built a monument in his honor on Front Street and requested that he be buried with his burro. When he passed away the following year, the town placed his ashes in the monument alongside Prunes.

The second monument honors a blind burro named Shorty. The story is that a local dog, named Bum, became Shorty's friend and would often follow him around town. When a car hit and killed Shorty, the town buried him on the courthouse lawn. Bum stayed near the grave until he died. He was buried next to Shorty, and the town placed a stone marker over the grave of the two best friends.

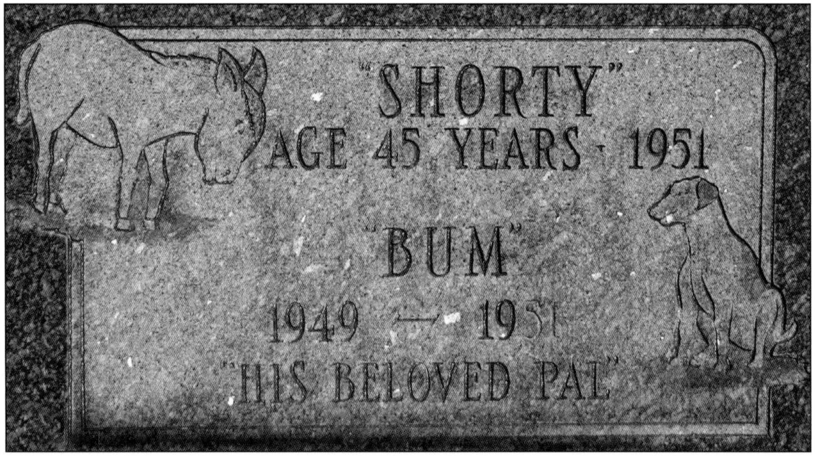
"SHORTY"
AGE 45 YEARS 1951
"BUM"
1949 — 1951
"HIS BELOVED PAL"
Monument in the town of Fairplay recognizing a famous friendship.

Burro Racing

Even though miners in the Rockies no longer use burros, the animals still play an important role in the town of Fairplay. Every year a few dozen runners and their burros race 30 miles to the summit of Mosquito Pass and back. Winners complete the course in about four hours—quite a feat when you consider that the starting point is at 9,953 feet, the top of Mosquito Pass is at 13,186 feet, and the burros are not always willing runners. The race has a 55-year tradition and brings around 10,000–15,000 visitors into the community of Fairplay, making it South Park's largest event.

Yellow wood violet

There are race rules. Each animal must carry a pack with a pick, shovel, and gold pan for a minimum load of 35 pounds. Competitors often add rocks to their load to meet the weight requirement. The burro's lead rope can be no longer than 15 feet, and the runner cannot lose control of the animal at any time during the race. There are now five burro races in Colorado, one in New Mexico, and one in Arizona. Fairplay bills its race as the planet's "highest, longest, roughest, and toughest." Prizes range from $1,000 to $5,000.

Looking out over the Gore Range.

Independence Pass

This view of Independence Pass covers 360 degrees!

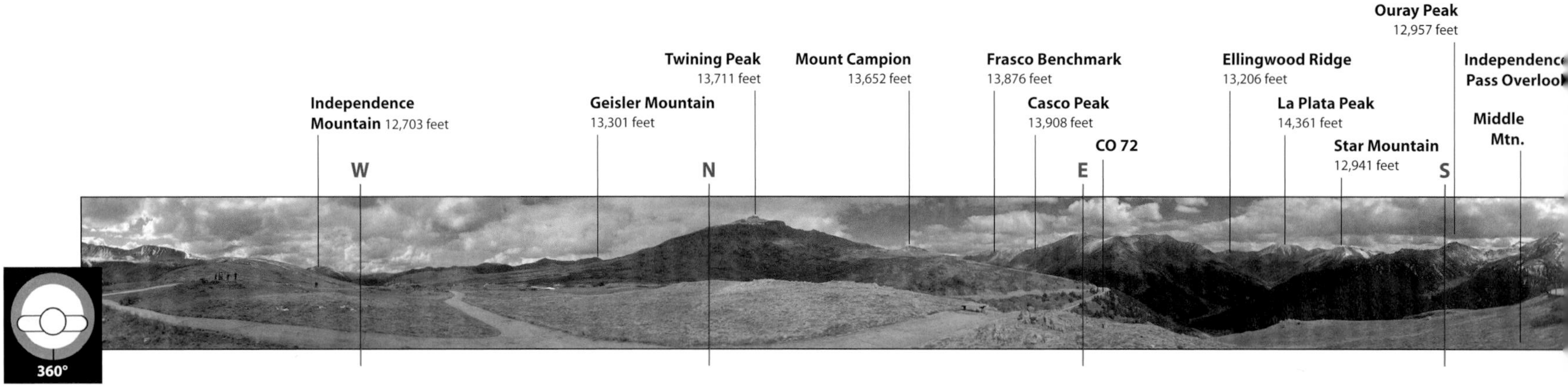
Ouray Peak
12,957 feet
Twining Peak
13,711 feet
Mount Campion
13,652 feet
Frasco Benchmark
13,876 feet
Ellingwood Ridge
13,206 feet
Independence Pass Overlook
Independence Mountain 12,703 feet
Geisler Mountain
13,301 feet
Casco Peak
13,908 feet
La Plata Peak
14,361 feet
Middle Mtn.
CO 72
Star Mountain
12,941 feet
W
N
E
S
360°

At the tundra-covered summit of **Independence Pass,** located in the Sawatch Mountains, the unobstructed view of distant peaks approaches 360 degrees. At 12,095 feet, this pass is the highest in Colorado. Runoff on the west side of the pass drains to the Roaring Fork River, while the east side empties into the North Fork of Lake Creek. The scenic drive along CO 82 from Twin Lakes to Aspen via Independence Pass is well worth the time.

The Colorado Department of Highways has found that it is too difficult to keep the pass open in the winter, although it is usually open by Memorial Day each year. The narrow road and tight turns restrict travel to vehicles less than 35 feet in length.

On the summit, a short trail winds down to an overlook of the valley to the south. Walking this trail offers a great opportunity to get a first-hand view of alpine tundra. A number of tundra ponds can be found on the summit. The careful observer will see thousands of insect larvae in these ponds during the warmest summer months.

Road construction and the numerous visitors to the summit have damaged much of this ecosystem. Tundra damage can take hundreds of years to recover. An Aspen-based foundation, The Independence Pass Foundation (IPF), works with local, state, and federal agencies on projects that maintain and enhance the Independence Pass corridor. Their restoration work can be seen in many disturbed areas, particularly on the west side of the pass.

Hunter's Pass

In 1881 B. Clark Wheeler built a toll road, named Hunter's Pass, over Independence Pass as a supply route and a way to export silver ore mined in the area. This became a preferred route because it allowed travelers to avoid the Ute Indians in the Roaring Fork Valley and Mount Sopris area. In addition, by crossing at Independence Pass, settlers avoided having to negotiate the narrow gorge of Glenwood Canyon north of Aspen.

When the gold mill in Independence closed in 1883, use of this toll road fizzled out. Four years later, railroads arrived in Aspen from

ORIGIN OF NAME	Named for a nearby mine that was staked on the Fourth of July in 1879.
ELEVATION	12,095 feet
NEARBY CITIES	Aspen/Twin Lakes
POINTS OF INTEREST	Town of Aspen, Aspen Ski Area, ghost town of Independence, Twin Lakes
COUNTY	Lake
HIGHWAY	CO 82/ Top of the Rockies
MILEPOST	61
GPS	39°06'32"N by 106°33'50"W
TOPO MAP	Independence Pass
GETTING THERE	**From Aspen,** travel east on CO 82 for 20 miles. **From Twin Lakes,** head west on CO 82 for 15 miles. Road closed in winter.

Scenic Byway

A snowstorm in September blankets Independence Pass. Visitors to the overlook ill-prepared for the 30-degree temperatures and 20-m.p.h winds, run back to the warmth of their cars.

A historic cabin at Independence Pass. The townsites and even the trash dumps of the mining camps of Colorado are considered archeological preserves and must not be disturbed.

the north and the road became defunct. The remains of the old road can still be found along the valley walls—one section is visible off the west side of the summit of the pass.

The Town of Independence

West of the summit and at the foot of the pass is the ghost town of Independence. The site, which is on the National Register of Historic Places, rests at 10,900 feet. One of the early prospectors in the area, Billy Belden, founded this mining town in 1879. It was known by many names in its short history. Locals knew it as Farwell, Sparkill, Mount Hope, Chipeta, and Mammoth City until the name Independence (the name of a nearby mine staked on July 4, 1879) finally stuck.

A major winter storm in 1899 completely cut off supplies to Independence and drove more than 100 miners out of town. They fashioned skis from the wood of their homes to make their way to Aspen. The last year-round resident of Independence moved out around 1912.

Twin Lakes

On the east side of the pass the traveler passes Twin Lakes and two towns, Twin Lakes Village and Interlaken. Twin Lakes Village, first settled in 1865, was once called Dayton. It was added to the National Historic Register in the 1970s.

Leadville's orchestra performed at Interlaken Resort every summer weekend during the resort's heyday.

Tourism developed quickly across Colorado at this time, and in 1885 the Interlaken Resort, in the town of Interlaken, was completed on the southern shore of the eastern Twin Lake. Like many resorts, it catered to the rich and famous, boasting a fancy restaurant and dance pavilion. Tourists could travel across the lake on a small steamboat named the *Idlewild.* Operating at 9,000 feet, it may have been the highest steamboat in the world. A five-horsepower engine powered the fifty-passenger, double-decked steamboat. Today, you can find the ruins of the historic Interlaken Resort by following the Colorado Trail along the south side of the lake from the trailhead that begins at its dam.

Bottles & Cans

Pieces of broken bottles and cans are commonly found around the old mining towns of the West. The law prohibits their removal, but more importantly, for the enjoyment of future generations, these items should be admired but left in place.

It is easy to take food preservation containers such as cans, plastic bottles, glass bottles, and plastic bags for granted nowadays, but in the late 1800s most of these containers did not exist. Food preservation was very difficult. Bottles and cans, the two existing food storage and preservation containers during the Gold Rush, were highly valued. They allowed food to be preserved for long periods of time and easily transported.

FOAM

SEALING
LOUISVILLE

Left: Bottles come in many shapes, sizes, and colors. Below: Many people collect bottles and cans, and there are numerous books and websites that describe the incredible variety that exist.

Making early bottles and cans was time consuming. Until the early 1800s, glass bottles were hand blown, shaped, and finished, one at a time. Even after glass blowers began using molds to shape multiple bottles at a time, they still needed to be hand finished. Early canners placed partially sealed containers of food into a boiling vat known as a water bath to sterilize the food and prevent spoiling. Both canned and bottled food was preserved this way.

The British Navy pioneered food storage in cans as early as 1813 when Peter Durand began making solid iron cans that often weighed more than the food they contained. The can was plated with tin to prevent rusting, hence the phrase "tin can." They were hand produced, one at a time. No one had a can opener in those years, so to get the food out of the container a person had to cut around the top near the outer edge with a hammer and chisel.

The distinctive top of this can dates it to the late 1800s

Thinner steel cans made an appearance in the 1860s. The production of these cans gave birth to the modern packaging industry.

The Maroon Bells on the west side of Independence Pass near Aspen are among the most photographed peaks in Colorado.

A Town Like No Other

Aspen's name alone invokes vivid mental images—celebrities, wealth, skiing, golf, beautiful mountain scenery, music, shopping, dining. However, the area was discovered and appreciated long before the rich and glamorous made it popular. The Ute Indians and their ancestors inhabited the area 8,000 years ago. When the first prospectors crossed over the pass from Leadville in the spring of 1879, they set up camp in the area, calling it Ute City. In the summer of 1880, Ute City had grown to 300 residents, and was renamed Aspen after the trees that covered the hillsides.

Above: An early "ski lift" on Aspen Mountain. Left: Today, people visit the former mining camp of Aspen to seek a different sort of gold: it is found in the fall in the form of aspen trees covering the hills.

These early prospectors discovered some of the richest lodes in the world buried beneath those hillsides, and Aspen soon surpassed Leadville to become the nation's largest producer of silver. In 1894, Aspen miners unearthed one of the largest nuggets of silver ever found—it weighed nearly 2,000 pounds!

By 1890, Aspen's 12,000 residents enjoyed the comforts of electric lights, two theaters, six newspapers, four schools, three banks, ten churches, many saloons, a hospital, and an opera house. Then, in 1893, silver was de-monetized and Aspen's mining economy crashed. Mines in the area shut down, and people turned to ranching and farming. The population dropped, and by the 1930s only 700 people lived there. Then, Aspen found a new calling; it opened its slopes to skiers.

In 1947 Aspen Mountain opened with the world's longest ski lift. Within a year they hosted an international competition, which eventually developed into the World Cup races. Three more ski resorts opened near the town in the next two decades: Buttermilk (1958), Aspen Highlands (1958), and Snowmass (1968). Aspen thus became a premiere international resort destination. Aspen has capitalized on its climate, recreation, history, and culture to develop into a year-round vacation hotspot.

Aspen's old-time feel adds to its charm as a tourist town. Many of the historic buildings and charming Victorian houses of Aspen still remain and have been restored to their original elegance. The Wheeler Opera House and the Hotel Jerome, built for Jerome B. Wheeler in 1889, are two excellent examples.

McClure Pass

The aspen around McClure Pass are some of the most spectacular in the state.

Whitehouse Mountain
11,975 feet
Mount Sopris
12,953 feet
Elk Mountain
11,826 feet
Treasure Mountain
13,528 feet
Chair Mountain
12,721 feet
Yule Quarry
N
E
S
217°

Twenty-four miles south of Carbondale and 8 miles south of Redstone on CO 133, travelers cross **McClure Pass.** It is not near any of the larger Colorado cities, and at only 8,763 feet it is one of the lowest passes in the state. You would never think about any of that when you take in the view to the southeast from near the summit, especially in the fall. The Elk Mountains to the east and south present a spectacular scene.

The pass separates the Crystal River drainage that flows north and the Gunnison River drainage that flows to the west. Both rivers eventually make their way to the Colorado River.

ORIGIN OF NAME	Thomas "Mack" McClure built a stage stop, known as the McClure House, on this pass around 1884.
ELEVATION	8,755 feet
NEARBY CITIES	Paonia/Redstone
POINTS OF INTEREST	Colorado Yule Marble Company, the Elk Mountains, Redstone Historic District, Redstone Castle
COUNTY	Gunnison
HIGHWAY	Road: CO 133/West Elk Loop
MILEPOST	43
GPS	39°07'44"N by 107°17'02"W
TOPO MAP	Placita
GETTING THERE	**From Paonia,** head east on CO 133 for 33 miles. **From Glenwood Springs,** take exit 116 off I-70 and head south on CO 82 for 12 miles to Carbondale. Turn south on CO 133 and continue 17 miles to Redstone. Continue south 9 miles.

Scenic Byway

Marble

While most miners were scouring the mountainsides of Colorado for gold and silver, George Yule, a mining engineer, found something a little different. In 1895, his marble quarry, dug into the east side of nearby Treasure Mountain, produced its first shipment. Ten years later, the Colorado Yule Marble Company formed from a stock issue of $2.5 million. The Yule Quarry produced stone used to construct the Lincoln Memorial; the Tomb of the Unknowns in Washington, D.C.; and the Colorado State Capitol building, as well as many other buildings and hundreds of statues.

The town of Marble incorporated in 1899 to meet the demands of Yule's mining business. It sits in a valley at 8,000 feet near the

Above: Snowshoeing on the Ragged Mountain Road off of McClure Pass. Right: Beaver ponds near the summit of McClure Pass.

Mine quarry site showing the mine buildings, a large crane anchored by cables to the quarry wall, and mine tram tracks. Photo by Louis Charles McClure, circa 1913.

headwaters of the Crystal River, about 6 miles south of McClure Pass on County Road 3. At one time, the remote Colorado Yule Marble Company employed nearly one thousand people. Though it terminated its full-time operations in 1941, fifty residents still call this scenic area their home.

Tomb of the Unknowns

Sculptors crafted the Tomb of the Unknowns at Arlington National Cemetery from the largest single block of marble ever quarried in the United States. Beginning in 1931, seventy-five men worked for more than a year to cut and remove it from the quarry. The block weighed in at 110 tons and measured 7'4" x 13'4" x 6'6" when it was finished.

The block of marble on the flatcar above became the Tomb of the Unknowns at Arlington Cemetery in Washington, D.C.

An aspen grove panorama on the west side of McClure Pass.

"The Ruby of the Rockies"

Redstone is a small community on the Crystal River at the base of McClure Pass. John Cleveland Osgood founded this town when he developed a significant mining empire in the area in the late 1800s. In 1892, Osgood's coal company merged with an iron and steel manufacturing company in Pueblo to form the Colorado Fuel and Iron Company (CF&I). CF&I, the largest employer in Colorado at the time, supplied most of the metal materials used in the construction of the railroads in the West.

At this time, the coal mining town of Redstone became a center of activity. Not only did mining take place in the area, but the company also produced high-grade coking coal in its beehive coking ovens.

Osgood, who employed 550 people, carried the reputation of both running a profitable mining enterprise and of working to improve the living conditions of the miners. He believed that if workers and their families enjoyed good living conditions they would be happy and would not strike. Osgood constructed the twenty-room Redstone Inn for the bachelors who worked for him, and eighty-four Swiss chalet–style homes for the married men. These structures included indoor plumbing and electricity, a true luxury for the times. The town of Redstone also included a school, a modern bathhouse, a theater, and a library.

Coking ovens still line the south entrance to the town of Redstone. Though these ovens are technologically obsolete, they now appear on the National Register of Historic Places. The town of Redstone is itself a Historic District because it is considered a rare,

Above: Twelve of the two hundred and forty-nine coke ovens at the town of Redstone. Left: Cleveholm Manor, also called the Redstone Castle, located just south of the town of Redstone and built by John Cleveland Osgood.

intact example of an industrial company town from the late 1800s. Original buildings in the town include worker's cottages and Osgood's large estate.

The Redstone Castle

After building his empire, Osgood built his private residence, called Cleveholm Manor, upstream from the town of Redstone. The Tudor-style home, known locally as the Redstone Castle and located on 150 acres, was built for the princely sum of $2.5 million ($52 million in today's dollars), and includes towers, turrets, and designer windows. Completed in 1902, it consisted of forty-two rooms, servant's quarters, a guardhouse, and carriage houses.

In 1903, during a stock war, John D. Rockefeller took over Osgood's mining company and ousted Osgood. The company shut down and the mines and coke ovens closed. Osgood dropped out of sight until he returned to Cleveholm Manor in 1925. He died soon after. Some say that his spirit still lights up cigars in his old home, and that the smoke can be smelled in its rooms.

The home, which has changed owners eight times, was listed on the National Register of Historic Places in 2004. Colorado Preservation, Inc., the National Trust for Historic Preservation, the Redstone Historical Society, and the Redstone Historic Preservation Commission have all worked to preserve Redstone Castle.

Kebler Pass

Looking north towards the Raggeds Wilderness from the Cliff Creek trailhead, west of Kebler Pass, on a crystal-clear fall day.

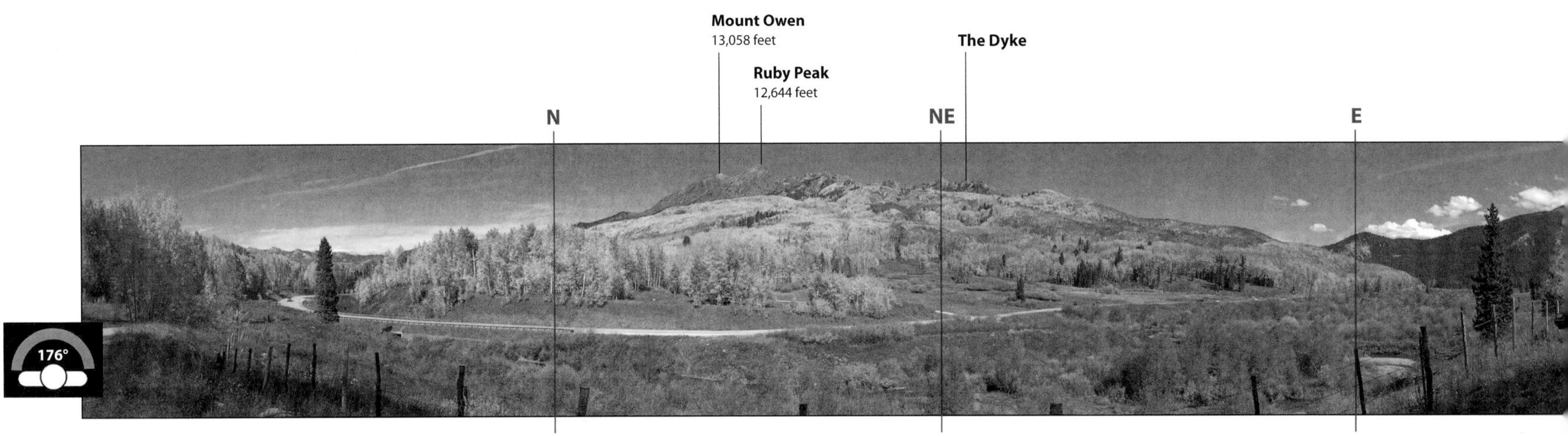
Mount Owen
13,058 feet
The Dyke
Ruby Peak
12,644 feet
N
NE
E
176°

No major roadway passes near this area, and **Kebler Pass** is open only during the summer, but it is well worth the time to explore. The well-graded dirt road, County Road 12, cuts through the largest stand of aspen trees in Colorado. In the summer some of the best wildflower gardens in the state grace the east side of the pass near the town of Crested Butte.

The Raggeds Wilderness, in White River and Gunnison National Forests, creates the magnificent view north of the Kebler Pass summit. Jagged, knife-edged ridges formed from intrusive volcanic dikes lend meaning to this wilderness area's name. The pleasantly

ORIGIN OF NAME	John Kebler owned the Colorado Fuel and Iron Company and many coal mines in the area.
ELEVATION	9,980 feet
NEARBY CITIES	Paonia/Crested Butte
POINTS OF INTEREST	Paonia Reservoir, Raggeds Wilderness
COUNTY	Gunnison
HIGHWAY	Gunnison 12/West Elk Loop
MILEPOST	20
GPS	38°50'59"N by 107°06'01"W
TOPO MAP	Mount Axtell
GETTING THERE	**From Paonia,** travel east on CO 133 for 16 miles. Turn south on County Road 12 and continue for 31 miles. **From Crested Butte,** travel west on Gunnison 12 for 7 miles.

Scenic Byway

Looking south toward the West Elk Wilderness across acres of aspen.

named Oh-Be-Joyful Pass, Creek, and Valley are on the eastern side of the wilderness area in the Ruby Range near the town of Crested Butte.

The original Kebler Pass road followed a Ute Indian trail. It was a private road before being taken over more than a hundred years ago by the State of Colorado. The state improved the road in 1930. It travels from Somerset, in the North Fork Valley near Paonia Reservoir, to the town of Crested Butte, and is named for John Kebler, who was president of the Colorado Fuel and Iron Company (CF&I). CF&I operated coal mines throughout much of southern Colorado, Wyoming, and Utah, as well as limestone quarries and mines for other materials that were important in the steelmaking process.

Homesteaders frequently utilized Kebler Pass Road to transport the potatoes they grew to the towns of Paonia and Hotchkiss. Cattle and sheep were herded along the road to railroad freight yards for shipment to the Denver stockyards. In 1893 the Denver & Rio Grande Railroad replaced Kebler Pass Road with tracks and began providing service to Crested Butte and to the mines around the summit of the pass. Kebler Pass, a town located at the pass's summit, served as a rail station.

Cemetery on a Summit

Kebler Pass is probably the only Colorado pass that has a marked cemetery on its summit. Only a few modern headstones have been placed there—piles or rings of rock or simply a slight rise in the

ground provide the only markings for most of the graves in the cemetery.

The cemetery served the community of Irwin, which was actually a collection of small mining camps located around the summit. Irwin's main street was over a mile long, with hotels, saloons, sawmills, stores, churches, a school, and a strong jail. Silver was discovered in Ruby Gulch in July 1879, and the district is often called the Irwin/Ruby mining district. The actual town of Ruby eventually merged with the town of Irwin. About $2 million in silver and gold came from the mines near this community. After a peak population of around 1,200 residents, the miners began to leave in late 1883 and all were gone within a year.

THE BRIGHT PROMISE OF
RUBY SILVER DREW 3000
PEOPLE TO THIS AREA IN
1879 FROM AS FAR AS
ENGLAND AND SCOTLAND
IRWIN BECAME A GHOST
TOWN WHEN SILVER WAS
DEMONETIZED IN 1884
THIS CEMETERY WAS
KNOWN AS RUBY CAMP
CEMETERY IN 1879
IT WAS RENAMED IRWIN
CEMETERY IN 1880
APPROXIMATELY 50
BURIALS WERE MADE
HERE BEFORE IT WAS
ABANDONED IN 1885

DIED
AGED

Right: Grave stones at the cemetery atop Kebler Pass.

Ferns grow in the shade of towering aspen in a grove on Kebler Pass.

Quaking Aspen!

The Colorado blue spruce is the state tree, but it is the quaking aspen that is the best known and most easily recognized tree in Colorado. The "gold rush" occurs every fall as millions of people are lured to the high country to view the beautiful colors of changing aspen. This member of the poplar family, which grows at elevations ranging from about 6,000 feet to almost 11,500 feet, can be found in all of Colorado's national forests—but nowhere in Colorado can one see as many acres of aspen as on the drive over Kebler Pass.

Quaking aspen, *Populus tremuloides*, gets its scientific name from a characteristic of the leaf. The heart-shaped leaves have a fine-toothed margin, and the petiole—the stem that attaches the leaf to

The spectrum of pigments in aspen leaves can be seen in this incredibly colorful stand at the base of McClure Pass.

the tree—is flattened. The flat petiole causes the leaf to quake or tremble in the slightest breeze. Many legends revolve around the belief that the tree trembles in the presence of man.

The color change in the high country starts in the middle of September and lasts into October, depending on temperatures and weather conditions. On a clear, cool September day, the combination of blue-gray and pure white of snow-capped peaks, yellow to red-colored aspen, and rich blue skies can easily cause a sensory overload.

The birdlike silhouette formed where a branch died and fell from the tree.

What causes this incredible fall show? All the gold, yellow, and red colors seen in aspen trees in the fall are present in the leaf throughout the spring and summer, too, but the predominant green chlorophyll necessary for food production overshadows them. When the length of the day decreases and temperatures drop in the fall, chlorophyll production slows down and eventually stops. The trees then begin to absorb the chlorophyll and leave behind the other pigments: Carotenoid pigments, which produce yellow, orange, and brown colors like those in carrots and corn; and Anthocyanin pigments, which produce the reds found in cranberries and red apples. Eventually, the dying leaves flutter to the ground in a rain of gold.

Temperature, the amount of seasonal moisture, and the amount of rain and snow in the fall all impact the time, duration, and intensity of the color changes. Adequate, but not excessive, summer moisture, cool nights without a freeze, and an absence of fall rains and snows produce the best fall shows. Here are some tips for finding the best fall colors:

- West facing slopes tend to display more vibrant colors
- Dry summers cause the leaves to dry out quickly and fall off the trees, while wet summers tend to make the leaves darken to brown or black and become moldy
- Trees at higher elevations, on north facing slopes, and those in the northern part of the state tend to change earlier than other trees

Aspen trees grow in a unique way called "cloning." What begins as one aspen becomes a whole grove when that tree's root system sends up "suckers," or shoots, which become new trees. This cloning produces huge areas of trees that all share the same root system. When you look at a grove of aspen trees, you are actually looking at one gigantic organism, all with the same genetic makeup connected to the same underground root structure. When fall begins, all the trees change colors at nearly the same time. This creates large expansive areas where all the trees are about the same color. This is even more obvious in the spring when all the trees in the stand leaf out at the same time.

Native tribes used aspens medicinally. They made tea to reduce fever using the bark, which contains a chemical similar to aspirin, and used a white powder found in the outer bark as sunscreen. Today, people use the wood of the tree for things like lettuce crates and wood chips. The wood grain makes beautiful ornamental items. Because it is a soft wood, it is not good for structural purposes.

Animals make use of the aspen tree, too. Beavers use aspen bark for food, and the wood and twigs for building dams and lodges. Elk, moose, and deer eat the bark, twigs, and foliage.

Aspen are sun-loving trees. They tend to grow in disturbed areas—often places where fires or logging operations have opened the forest floor

Marcellina Mountain in the Raggeds Wilderness.

to full sunlight. As a grove grows, the branches on the lower parts of the inner trees do not receive enough sunlight and therefore do not produce leaves. These branches die off and fall from the tree, leaving a characteristic mark like the silhouette of a flying bird. The tree continues to grow straight up, losing more branches. This produces a tall thin trunk topped by a crown of leaves. Eventually the tree reaches a height where nutrients, picked up from the soil by its roots, can no longer efficiently reach its top. The interior wood then begins to rot, and the tree begins to die. The maximum age of these trees is a little over a hundred years.

Since the aspen trees shade the floor of the forest, no new aspen can grow beneath them. They are therefore replaced over time with shade-loving trees—in this region, generally fir or spruce—that can grow in their shadow. Eventually the spruce and fir trees become the dominant vegetation. The aspen will return if fire or logging destroys the forest and produces open areas where they can grow in full sunlight.

Most of the huge expanses of aspen across Colorado are actually the result of logging activity or fires caused by careless miners over a hundred years ago. Today, environmental consciousness is reducing logging activity and man can now prevent as well as fight forest fires. This is actually leading to a decline in the number and size of aspen groves across the state. There has been a seemingly unrelated die-off in aspen groves across the Rocky Mountain West in recent years, the cause of which is not fully understood.

Tons of Coal

Some of the world's best quality coal comes from the North Fork Valley of the Gunnison River near Kebler Pass. Billions of tons of coal still remain in underground beds stretching from there to eastern Utah. This coal provided an important incentive to the railroads' westward expansion because of its value as a fuel not only for locomotives, but also for the iron mills that produced the rails, spikes, and engine parts for the trains and their tracks. Mining near Crested Butte and in the Somerset coalfield began in the early 1900s. Coal is still mined from the Kebler Pass area.

Between 1902 and 1974, nine mines operated in the Somerset coalfield. Coal mining was such a big enterprise in Somerset that the Utah Fuel Company once owned the entire town, including its houses, schools, stores, and saloons. The town's diverse ethnic makeup, like that of many mining towns, created language barriers, unique cultural differences, and racial friction. Even with these difficulties, miners were, and are, a family when underground. They take care of each other because their lives depend on it.

Cottonwood Pass

View looking northwest toward Taylor Park with the Elk and West Elk Mountains in the distance.

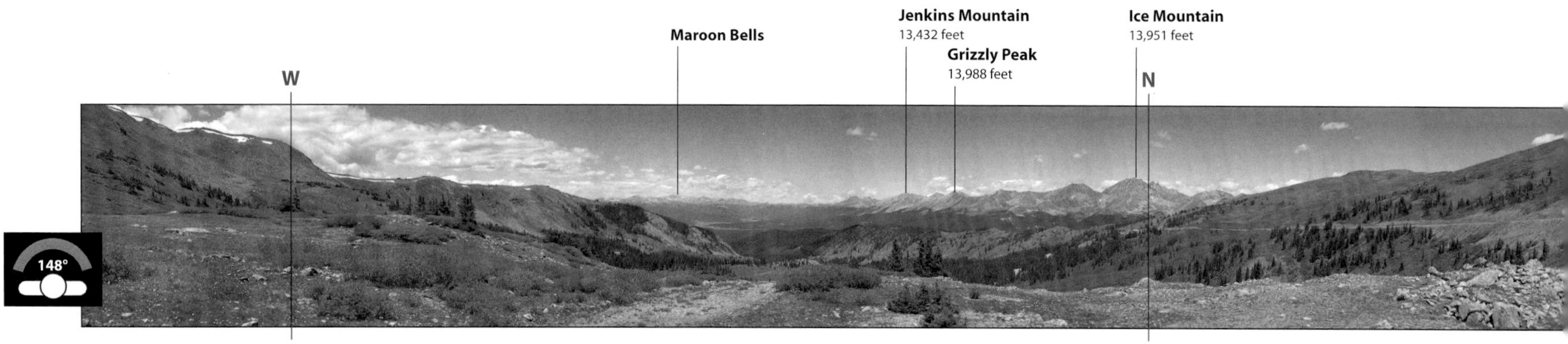
Maroon Bells
Jenkins Mountain
13,432 feet
Grizzly Peak
13,988 feet
Ice Mountain
13,951 feet
W
N
148°

Cottonwood Pass, located about 21 miles west of the town of Buena Vista, is one of three passes named "Cottonwood" accessible by car in Colorado. The other two are near the towns of Gypsum and Fraser, respectively. A good look at the area around the summit of this 12,126-foot pass will convince you that this has been a natural route for many travelers through the ages. The remnants of many old trails and wagon roads crisscross the summit.

The Ute created a trail over this pass while traveling between the hot springs on its east side and their hunting grounds on its west side. In 1859, prospectors who panned for gold in Taylor Park,

located west of the pass, undoubtedly used their route. With the discovery of silver in Taylor Park in later years, wagon roads crossed the pass to provide access to the mines there. After mining traffic in Taylor Park died out, people still used the pass to reach Aspen, but when railroads reached the town via a different route in 1887, use of Cottonwood Pass died out. Some reports say the last stagecoach crossed it in 1911.

Tourism brought travelers back into the Cottonwood Pass area in 1959. It was around this time that the U.S. Forest Service, along with Gunnison and Chaffee counties, built the current road over the pass. Chaffee County paved the east side in 1990, but the west side remains a well-graded dirt road.

ORIGIN OF NAME	The lanceleaf cottonwood is a type of poplar tree found in the river valleys throughout Colorado.
ELEVATION	12,126 feet
NEARBY CITIES	Gunnison/Buena Vista
POINT OF INTEREST	Taylor Park Reservoir
COUNTY	Chaffee
HIGHWAY	Forest Route 209, County Road 340
MILEPOST	n/a
GPS	38°49'40"N by 106°24'33"W
TOPO MAP	Tincup
GETTING THERE	**From Gunnison,** travel north on CO 135 for 11 miles to Almont. Turn east on County Road 742 for 20 miles to reach Taylor Park Reservoir. Turn east on County Road 209 and continue 18 miles. **From Buena Vista,** head west on County Road 306 for 21 miles.

202°

View looking south down Cottonwood Creek. The paved section of the Cottonwood Pass Road climbs to the pass summit on the right.

130°

View looking down South Texas Creek toward the Collegiate Peaks Wilderness.

Mount Princeton Hot Springs near Buena Vista at the base of 14,197-foot Mount Princeton.

Taylor Park Reservoir

Taylor Park Reservoir now fills much of Taylor Park. The Federal Bureau of Reclamation built the dam creating the reservoir in 1935 to 1937. Interestingly, Taylor Park and Taylor River are named after a Jim Taylor of Glenwood Springs, one of the first prospectors to discover gold in the area, while the Taylor Dam and Taylor Park Reservoir are named after Congressman Edward Taylor, who was instrumental in the reservoir development.

Hot Springs in Colorado

The Colorado Geological Survey lists 93 hot springs and geothermal wells across the state. Some communities even heat private, public, and town structures with geothermal heat. Most of the

A creek cascades through a Colorado forest.

springs emit a distinct sulfur-like odor because of the water's high concentration of hydrogen sulfide. Many of these springs have provided a stable quantity of water, chemistry, and temperature for hundreds of years. The Ute and other Native Americans enjoyed the mineral-rich mud or water's curative powers for many ailments, just as we do today. There is documentation of tribal battles over rights to hot springs.

In the late 1850s, many visitors—some of them famous—came to Colorado specifically to enjoy the hot springs, but during the mid-twentieth century, interest in mineral baths faded. This interest has revived, however, in the last few years, encouraging a number of Colorado sites to improve their facilities to attract new visitors. Campgrounds, hotels, and large swimming pools are often found at the sites. The world's largest hot springs pool is in Glenwood Springs.

Some of the best known developed Colorado sites include hot springs in the towns of Salida, Buena Vista, Moffat, Mount Princeton, Nathrop, Durango, Glenwood Springs, Hot Sulphur Springs, Idaho Springs, Ouray, Pagosa Springs, Steamboat Springs, and Telluride. Humans have enjoyed these hot springs for thousands of years.

Cascades off Mt. Princeton on the east side of Cottonwood Pass.

Monarch Pass

30

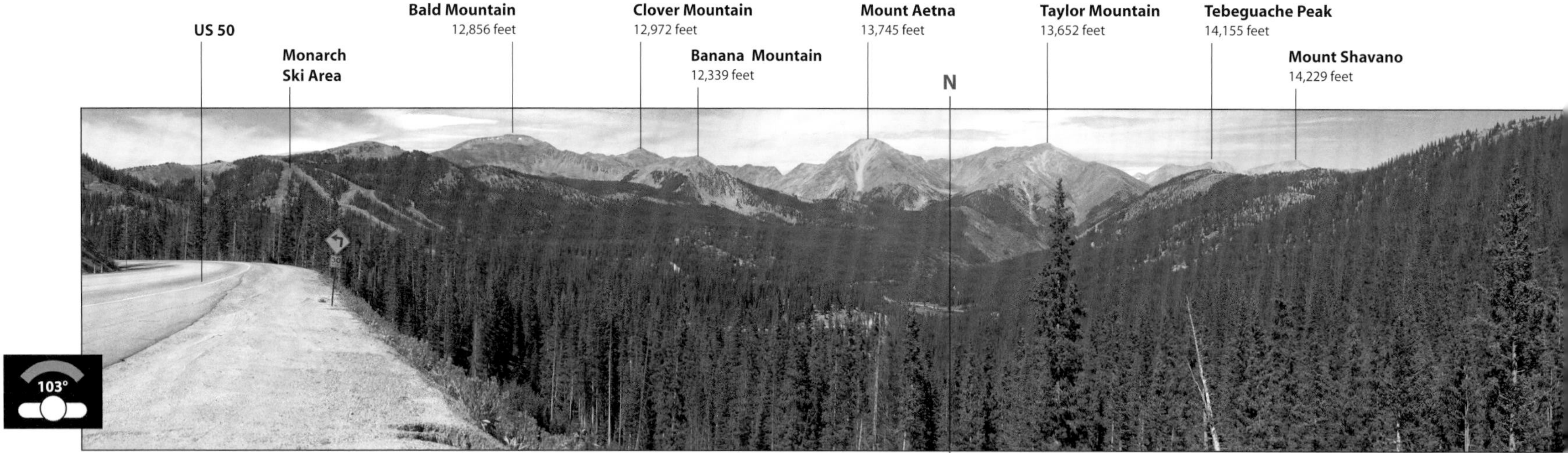
US 50
Monarch Ski Area
Bald Mountain 12,856 feet
Clover Mountain 12,972 feet
Banana Mountain 12,339 feet
Mount Aetna 13,745 feet
N
Taylor Mountain 13,652 feet
Tebeguache Peak 14,155 feet
Mount Shavano 14,229 feet
103°

Monarch Pass straddles the Continental Divide 23 miles west of the town of Salida. It is the only Colorado pass that has a commercial tourist operation other than a gift shop located on its summit. Departing from Monarch Pass and ascending 700 feet to an elevation of 12,012 feet, The Monarch Crest Scenic Tram offers visitors sprawling Rocky Mountain views, which include Pikes Peak and the Continental Divide. Built in 1966, the tramway begins at a large gift shop located atop the pass.

ORIGIN OF NAME	The Monarch Mine was an early claim in the area and the name was later applied to other area features.
ELEVATION	11,312 feet
NEARBY CITIES	Gunnison/Salida
POINTS OF INTEREST	Continental Divide, Pikes Peak view, Monarch Crest Scenic Tram
COUNTY	Chaffee
HIGHWAY	US 50
MILEPOST	199.5
GPS	38°29'48"N by 106°19'32"W
TOPO MAP	Pahlone Peak
GETTING THERE	**From Gunnison,** drive east on US 50 for 42 miles. **From Salida,** drive west on US 50 for 23 miles.

View looking northeast from Old Monarch Pass.

The Monarch and Little Charm silver mines were staked on what was once called Limestone Mountain and later renamed Monarch Hill. To reach the mines, Hugh and Sam Boone constructed the Monarch Pass Toll Road in 1880. They later extended it to the Tomichi and White Pine mining camps farther west in Gunnison County.

The original route over Monarch Pass goes through what is now the Monarch Mountain ski area. Maps still call it Old Monarch Pass. It is a well-maintained dirt road that can be accessed off US 50, just east of the summit of Monarch Pass. Though the first few hundred yards of the road are very steep, the views from just above the summit are spectacular and well worth the trip.

The current route over the pass was completed in 1939 and, at 11,312 feet, is the high point for US 50. At over 3,000 miles long, US 50 is one of the longest highways in the United States. A July

1997 *Time Magazine* article called it "the backbone of America." It is also known as "The Loneliest Road in America."

Skiing

The city of Salida constructed the Monarch Pass Ski Area, on the east side of the pass, with the help of the Works Project Administration (WPA), a program President Franklin Roosevelt initiated in 1935 to reduce unemployment during the Great Depression. They completed the ski area in December 1939 and dedicated it as the Monarch Winter Sports Area in February 1940. It is now called Monarch Mountain.

Looking west from Old Monarch Road toward Gunnison and the West Elk Mountains.

Indian Paintbrush: A Palette of Color!

The palette of color for Indian paintbrush includes an incredible range. The name "paintbrush" could not be more appropriate. The bright colors of the paintbrush are not actually its flowers—they are bracts, or leaf-like structures, around the flowers. The flower itself is a pale green spike hidden in the bracts. Since the leaves contain the color, it appears that the plant blooms for an entire summer!

Indian paintbrush grows in North and Central America, Asia, and the Andes. The majority of species grow in the West, but some are found in the central portion of the U.S. and on the East Coast. Habitats include grasslands, deserts, woodland shrub, and bogs. A very short yellow version is common on the alpine tundra.

The plant actually depends on other plants for survival—it is a parasite and therefore unable to survive alone in the soil. A tissue that grows from its roots takes water and nutrients from the roots of other plants, such as grass, sagebrush, and buckwheat. For this reason paintbrush are seldom successfully grown in flower gardens. Some gardeners have been successful when they plant them with a clump of blue grama grass as a host plant.

Did you know . . .

- Common names include painted cup, prairie-fire, and painted lady
- The genus name, *Castillejo*, refers to Prof. Domingo Castillejo, an eighteenth-century instructor of botany at Cadiz, Spain
- Paintbrush is a member of the snapdragon family
- The 200 species in the western United States are difficult to differentiate—they hybridize, making them highly variable in color and shape

Poncha Pass

Looking northwest from the summit of Poncha Pass.

Mount Ouray
13,971 feet
Chipeta Mountain
13,472 feet
W
Carbonate Mountain
13,663 feet
Tebeguache Peak
14,155 feet
Mount Shavano
14,229 feet
Mount Antero
14,269 feet
NW
Mount Princeton
14,197 feet
87°

Poncha Pass is the lowest pass listed on the *Official Map to Colorado* and can actually be seen when looking down from one area of Marshall Pass to the west. From the summit of Poncha Pass, US 285 southbound travels down into the largest valley in the state, the San Luis Valley.

The name of the pass has been through some variations. Take your pick from Poncha, Poncho, Puncha, Puntia, Punita, Puncho, and Punche. All of these names appear in the literature, maps, and newspapers of the area. No one really knows where the name Poncha Pass

ORIGIN OF NAME	Unknown, but possibly from the Spanish word for "mild" since it is an easy pass to cross, or a Ute word that means footpath.
ELEVATION	9,010 feet
NEARBY CITIES	Saguache/Poncha Spgs
POINTS OF INTEREST	Sangre de Cristo Range, San Luis Valley
COUNTY	Chaffee
HIGHWAY	US 285
MILEPOST	119
GPS	38°25'20"N by 106°05'13"W
TOPO MAP	Poncha Pass
GETTING THERE	**From Saguache,** travel north on US 285 for 35 miles.
	From Poncha Springs, travel south on US 285 for 7 miles.

Above: Looking south from the summit of Poncha Pass with the Sangre de Cristo Range on the left of the highway. Left: A Denver & Rio Grande Western narrow gauge train traveling north near Villa Grove. This stretch of 52 miles of the straightest track in the Colorado mountains is framed by the Sangre de Cristo Range to the east.

came from. Some believe it originated from a Ute Indian word for footpath that no one knew how to write in English. Others claim that it's a derivation of any number of Spanish or Indian words for things like belly, sag, footpath, low point, mild, gentle, easy, warmth, warm spring, cape, and tobacco.

Trappers passed through the Poncha Pass area in the early 1800s looking for beaver. Gold was reported at the pass in 1868, prompting Otto Mears to build the Poncha Pass Wagon Road the following year. He sold it to the Denver & Rio Grande Railroad in 1880. Railroads crossed the pass until 1950. The railroad line going south

from Poncha was the longest stretch of straight track in the Colorado mountains—it went 52 miles without a curve.

Saguache

On the south side of Poncha Pass, the town of Saguache sits where two forks of the Old Spanish Trail once converged. The Spanish explored much of this area when it was part of Spain's New World Empire. Explorers and traders used the Spanish Trail because it was so well documented. Wagon roads and trains followed as more people settled the West. Most of the area around Saguache relies on agriculture as its economic base. Some of its ranches have been worked continuously since the late 1800s.

A Valley and Three Mountain Ranges

The San Luis Valley, the largest valley in Colorado, covers about 8,000 square miles—an area about the size of Connecticut. It has an average elevation of 7,500 feet and spans both Colorado and New Mexico.

The Sangre de Cristo Range begins at Poncha Pass and continues along the east side of the San Luis Valley for 200 miles, ending where it hits Glorieta Pass in New Mexico. The Spanish explorer Antonio Valverde y Cosio named the Sangre de Cristo Mountains in 1719 after seeing the reddish hue of the snowy peaks at sunrise. The name translates to mean "Blood of Christ."

The San Juan Mountains form the west side of the San Luis Valley. They cover over 12,000 square miles of southwestern Colorado and are one of the highest and most rugged ranges in North America. Hundreds of the San Juan peaks exceed 13,000 feet, and many are over 14,000 feet. The San Juan's are probably the most remote and inaccessible mountain range in Colorado.

To the north of Poncha Pass is the Sawatch range, which is about seventy miles long. The Sawatch Mountains tend to be high and massive, but because of their gentle contours, most are easy to climb. The range is on the Continental Divide and has fifteen fourteeners, more than any other range in Colorado. In addition, four of Colorado's five highest peaks are in the Sawatch Range.

Marshall Pass

Looking east down Poncha Creek from the summit of Marshall Pass.

E
Mount Ouray
13,971 feet
Sangre de Cristo
Mountains
100°

The **Marshall Pass** road, which is dirt and well graded, travels around the south side of Mount Ouray, at the southern end of the Sawatch Mountains. This scenic route offers good views of the 13,971-foot mountain, named for the Ute Chief Ouray. Chipeta Mountain, located a mile northwest of Mount Ouray, is named for the chief's wife.

The roadbed follows the narrow gauge transcontinental railroad line that once connected Denver with Salt Lake City. A Denver & Rio Grande Railroad helper station was located at the western foot of Marshall Pass in Sargent. Helper engines—locomotives that temporarily assist trains requiring additional power to climb a grade—were added to eastbound trains at this location to help the trains cross over Marshall Pass. About all that remains of structures associated with the railroad over Marshall Pass is a water tank in the town of Sargent.

Looking east from Marshall Pass Road.

A Major Toothache

Marshall Pass is named for a man with a toothache. In 1873 Lt. William L. Marshall was surveying the San Juan area for the Wheeler Survey. His party was camped near present-day Silverton when the weather turned bad and threatened to strand the expedition. The group decided to return to Denver via its regular route over Cochetopa Pass.

On the return trip, Marshall developed a toothache so severe that he was unable to eat solid foods. His blacksmith offered to pull the tooth, but Marshall would not allow it, preferring instead to return to Denver to see a regular dentist. To speed up the trip, he set out to find a shortcut. He and his packer left the main survey party and

ORIGIN OF NAME	Lt. William L. Marshall discovered this pass while surveying with the United States Geographical Surveys.
ELEVATION	10,882 feet
NEARBY CITIES	Sargent/Salida
POINTS OF INTEREST	Salida, Poncha Springs, Colorado Trail
COUNTY	Saguache
HIGHWAY	NF 200, NF 243.2
MILEPOST	16.5
GPS	38°23'29"N by 106°14'50"W
TOPO MAP	Mount Ouray
GETTING THERE	**From Sargents** on US 50, travel east on Forest Route 243 for 19 miles. **From Salida,** travel west for 5 miles on US 50. Turn south on US 285 and travel 5 miles to NF 200/Marshall Pass Rd. Continue for 10 miles.

headed north with the intent of crossing the Continental Divide near what is now Independence Pass.

Snow blocked the route so he decided to follow a gap that he had found earlier. They ascended what is now Marshall Pass, and he immediately realized it could make an ideal route for a road or railroad. Not wanting to waste the opportunity, he continued his survey even through his severe pain. He and the packer made it to Denver (and his dentist) four days before the main party and saved about 125 miles in the process. The dentist did remove the tooth.

Early Roads

In 1877 Otto Mears developed the route as a toll road to connect the Arkansas River drainage on the east to the Gunnison watershed on the west. The Denver & Rio Grande Railroad bought Mears's toll road for $13,000 and built its narrow-gauge railroad west over the pass. The first train on this route reached Gunnison in August of 1881, crossing the Continental Divide at 10,846 feet. Snow sheds were built at the summit of this and many other passes, where high winds made it impossible to keep the tracks clear during blizzardy winter months.

Passenger service over Marshall Pass ended in 1940, but the line continued to carry freight, including livestock from Gunnison Country and coal from Crested Butte. However, trucks began hauling the livestock and the coal mine closed, and the railroad abandoned the line in 1953. It removed the rails in 1955. The grade became a county road in 1956. Now, it is well graded, but not kept open in the winter.

Top: Looking south from the summit of Marshall Pass at a train pulling out of one of the snow sheds that were located on the summit. Above: The same location today.

MARSHALL PASS AND MT OURAY
Colorado Historical Society

Top: A view of the west side of Marshall Pass, with Mount Ouray in the background. Right: This photo was taken from approximately the same location today.

Top: A Denver & Rio Grande water tank in the town of Sargents on the west side of Marshall Pass. Above: Aspen frame Marshall Pass Road.

Interior view of a timber-supported snow shed that once stood on Marshall pass.

The Colorado Trail

A section of the Colorado Trail crosses the summit of Marshall Pass. In 1973 the United States Forest Service envisioned a premier, scenic trail system for individuals and families who enjoyed the outdoors but did not want an extreme wilderness experience. In 1974 several focus groups organized to brainstorm and develop a trail plan. The Colorado Mountain Trails Foundation was formed.

The group identified three goals: 1) to develop a main trail between Denver and Durango and provide access trails and loops to points of interest off this main trail; 2) to provide educational opportunities for schools, universities, and organizations in an outdoor classroom setting; and 3) to provide for public involvement, awareness, and appreciation of resource management, and to encourage public participation in voluntary construction, maintenance, and management of the trail.

The Colorado Mountain Trails Foundation and the forest service developed a continuing relationship to build and maintain the Colorado Trail. In the 1980s the Colorado Mountain Club's Trail and Hut Committee joined the effort. This was a turning point for the Colorado Trail. The plan now relied on volunteers, which allowed the trail to be built at a cost of about $500 a mile.

Colorado governor Richard Lamm offered his support, which improved cooperation between the state of Colorado and the forest service. A new nonprofit organization, The Colorado Trail Foundation, assumed responsibility for building the trail. The summers of 1986 and 1987 saw completion of the trail between Denver and Durango.

The trail is made up of 28 segments, covers a distance of 482.9 miles, and gains a total of 74,975 feet, reaching a low of 5,520 feet in Waterton Canyon and a high of 13,240 feet on Coney Summit in the San Juan Mountains. It crosses, or comes close to Tennessee Pass, Kenosha Pass (pg. 124), Marshall Pass (pg. 176), Spring Creek Pass, and Molas Pass (pg. 204) on its way across the state. It crosses the Continental Divide over fifty times. The Colorado Trail was built entirely by a volunteer effort, and volunteers continue to maintain it. For volunteer work vacation opportunities on the Colorado Trail visit www.coloradotrail.org.

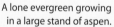

A lone evergreen growing in a large stand of aspen.

Looking west from near the summit of Marshall Pass.

Dallas Divide

Looking south toward the Mount Sneffels Wilderness.

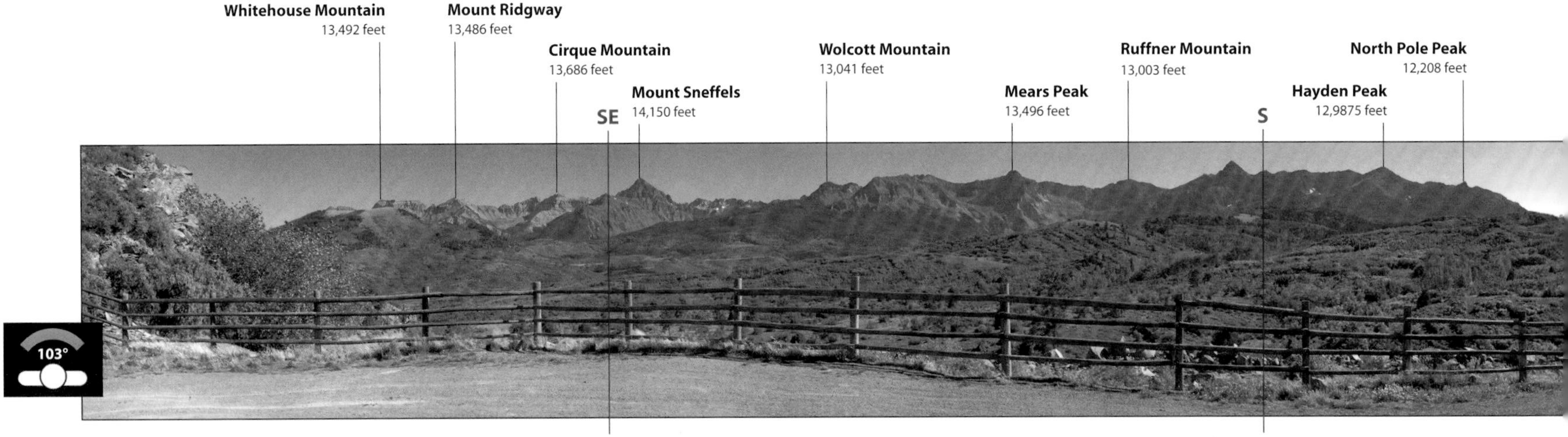
Whitehouse Mountain
13,492 feet
Mount Ridgway
13,486 feet
Cirque Mountain
13,686 feet
SE
Mount Sneffels
14,150 feet
Wolcott Mountain
13,041 feet
Mears Peak
13,496 feet
Ruffner Mountain
13,003 feet
S
Hayden Peak
12,9875 feet
North Pole Peak
12,208 feet
103°

The sweeping, postcard vistas from this divide serve up calendar material year after year. **Dallas Divide** gets its name from George Mifflin Dallas, the same man for whom Dallas, Texas was named. Dallas served as vice president of the United States from 1845 to 1849 under Democratic President James K. Polk. The divide is about 9 miles west of the town of Ridgway on US 62, the San Juan Skyway.

Fathers Francisco Atanasio Dominquez and Francisco Silvestre Velez de Escalante were probably the first Europeans in the area. They led a twelve-man expedition across the divide in 1776, on their way to explore what is now western Colorado. Their route later became part of the Old Spanish Trail.

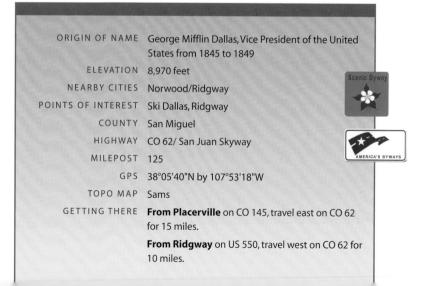

ORIGIN OF NAME	George Mifflin Dallas, Vice President of the United States from 1845 to 1849
ELEVATION	8,970 feet
NEARBY CITIES	Norwood/Ridgway
POINTS OF INTEREST	Ski Dallas, Ridgway
COUNTY	San Miguel
HIGHWAY	CO 62/ San Juan Skyway
MILEPOST	125
GPS	38°05'40"N by 107°53'18"W
TOPO MAP	Sams
GETTING THERE	**From Placerville** on CO 145, travel east on CO 62 for 15 miles. **From Ridgway** on US 550, travel west on CO 62 for 10 miles.

© Colorado Historical Society

Left: Photo by William Henry Jackson of the Dallas Divide. Above: Looking east from Dallas Divide toward the Uncompahgre Wilderness.

In 1882, Otto Mears opened a toll road over the pass, providing access to Telluride. He laid track there for his Rio Grande Southern Railroad in 1889 and 1890. In 1953, those tracks were abandoned. The highway straddling the divide today, CO 62, follows Mears' original railroad route.

Ridgway

Ridgway, originally called Magentie and later Dallas Junction, is an excellent example of an old railroad town, with a variety of railroad-era buildings and homes. The town, founded in 1890 by Otto Mears, was a major hub of railroad activity in the area, serving mining camps all around the San Juan Mountains. It was the headquarters and northern terminus for Mears' Rio Grande Southern Railroad. The depot there also served the Denver & Rio Grande Railroad, founded by General William Jackson Palmer, which ran narrow gauge track from Montrose into Ouray by way of Ridgway. In 1976 the last freight train from Montrose to Ridgway ran over the Denver & Rio Grande Railroad tracks, ending nearly a century of railroad service. Railroad history, however, still lives on in Ridgway.

Ridgway it is often misspelled "Ridgeway" on maps and other documents. Even residents have been known to misspell it. It was named for Robert M. Ridgway, a division superintendent for the Denver & Rio Grande Railroad.

Small mining cars once carried ore out of the mines in the area.

A Hollywood Star

Westerns were a popular movie genre in the 1950s and '60s. Ridgway's western flavor and beautiful San Juan Mountain backdrop made it an ideal Hollywood filming location. The town "co-starred" in many movies, including, *A Tribute to a Bad Man* (1956), with James Cagney; *How the West Was Won* (1962), with Debbie Reynolds and Gregory Peck; and, *True Grit* (1969), starring John Wayne, Glenn Campbell, and Kim Darby.

Ski Dallas

People used to ski in Dallas—Dallas, Colorado, that is. The ski area, Ski Dallas, was just west of the Dallas Divide summit and as basic as it gets. The only lifts that Ski Dallas offered were a rope tow and a T-Bar. The area also offered one ski patrolman, a ski school, rentals, and a small concession stand. Since the owners and operators had other jobs, it operated only on weekends. Locals worked a couple of hours a day to get "comp" ski tickets. The area opened at night when a full moon prevailed.

Ski Dallas operated from 1960 to 1974. Many locals learned to ski at Ski Dallas, but the number of gloves they went through using the rope tow probably offset what they saved on lift tickets.

When most people think of skiing in Colorado they think of Vail, Copper, Aspen, Telluride, Winter Park, and the twenty-some others currently operating. In the early days of the Colorado ski industry, around 140 ski areas operated, but most are only a memory.

Above: Corrals and stockpens along the abandoned railroad grade south of the summit of Dallas Divide.

Lizard Head Pass

Looking east from above the parking lot on the summit of Lizard Head Pass.

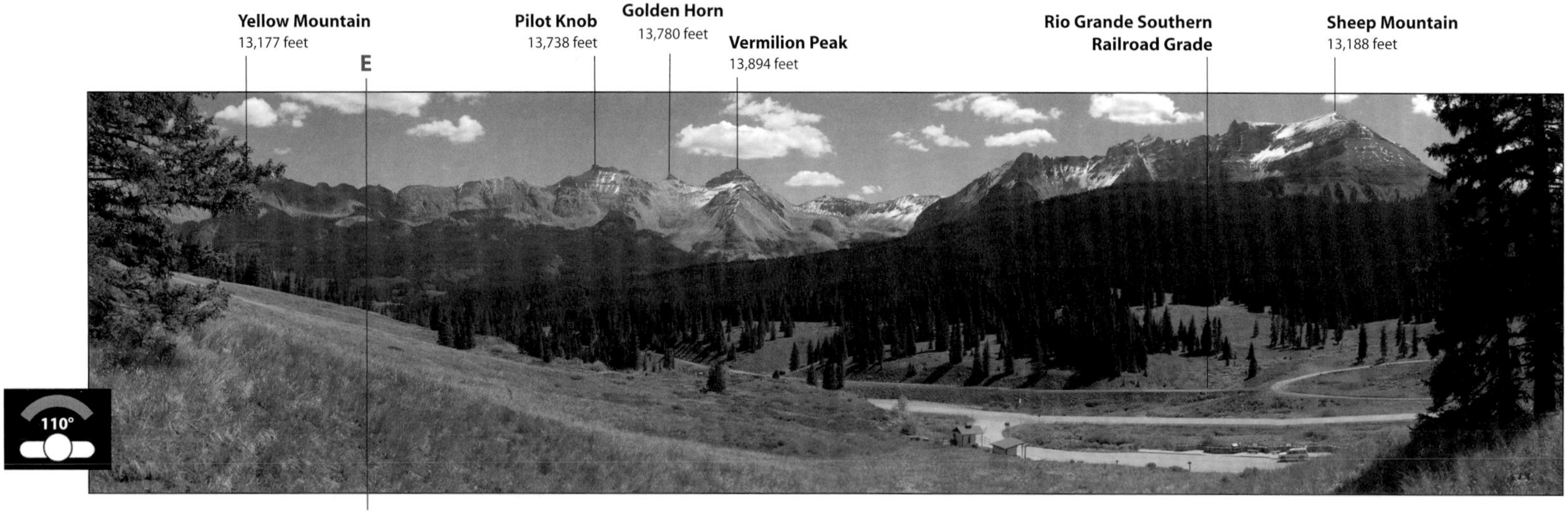
Yellow Mountain
13,177 feet
E
Pilot Knob
13,738 feet
Golden Horn
13,780 feet
Vermilion Peak
13,894 feet
Rio Grande Southern
Railroad Grade
Sheep Mountain
13,188 feet
110°

The spectacular San Juan Mountains, one of the most beautiful mountain ranges in Colorado, surround what was the highest point on the Rio Grande Southern Railroad. Located in a meadow 16 miles south of Telluride, **Lizard Head Pass** was once home to a railroad siding, a wye, stockpens, a depot, and a bunkhouse. During the summer, it was an active shipping point for livestock.

Today, you can find interpretive signs at the summit parking lot that contain information about the Rio Grande Southern Railroad. Remnants of an old snow shed that once stretched 1,549 feet to cover the railroads siding and wye can also be seen at the pass.

Lizard head Mountain, at 13,113 feet, is located northwest of the pass.

ORIGIN OF NAME	A peak located northwest of the pass is said to look like a lizard's head.
ELEVATION	10,222 feet
NEARBY CITIES	Dolores/Telluride
POINTS OF INTEREST	Telluride Ski Resort, Ames Hydroelectric Generating Plant
COUNTY	San Miguel
HIGHWAY	CO 145/San Juan Skyway
MILEPOST	145
GPS	37°48'40"N, 107°54'22"W
TOPO MAP	Mount Wilson
GETTING THERE	**From Dolores,** travel north on CO 145 for 49 miles. **From Telluride,** travel south on CO 145 for 16 miles.

The pass gained its name from a nearly 400-foot-high rock formation visible from the pass, which is said to look like a lizard's head. A circa 1890 report of an earthquake in the area may have been rock falling from this feature. It no longer looks like a lizard, if it ever did. This rock formation was used as the logo of the Rio Grande Southern Railroad's Silver San Juan Scenic Line.

World's First Alternating Current Hydroelectric Plant

At the foot of the north side of Lizard Head Pass, a small hydroelectric plant sits in the tiny community of Ames. The Ames Hydroelectric Generating Plant, built in 1891, was the first alternating current hydroelectric plant in the world. At the time, gold miners were struggling to supply electricity to their mines as fuel for steam power became more and more difficult to obtain. All the trees in the area had been cut, and the high price of coal—$40 to $50 a ton—was becoming prohibitive.

AMES STATION
WORLD'S FIRST GENERATING STATION
TO PRODUCE AND TRANSMIT
ALTERNATING CURRENT

Above: The Ames power plant in 2007. Right: An old fence below the town of Ames with the Mount Sneffels Wilderness in the distance.

STOP

Construction of the water-powered plant began in the summer of 1890. A generator and a motor from the Westinghouse Company were installed that winter. They diverted water from Lake Fork of the San Miguel River, which ran a few hundred feet above the power plant, to propel a waterwheel that was connected by a belt to the generator.

The 3000 volts of electricity produced at the plant were transmitted 2.6 miles to the Gold King Mine above Ophir to power the motor-driven mill that crushed the ore mined there. The plant required fifteen to twenty employees, and its entire electrical output was dedicated to mining operations. The savings were enormous. This power plant provided the mine with all the electricity it needed for $500 per month, while a coal-fuel plant would have cost $2,500 per month.

Power for all the mines in the Telluride area eventually came from the Ames plant, and by 1894 it had become a model worldwide for the generation and transmission of electric power. Telluride,

Above: Rio Grande Southern freight train southbound on Lizard Head Pass in 1945. Left: The same location in 2007.

called the "City of Lights" at the time, became the first town in the world to have electric street lamps.

A wooden shed housed the Ames Power Plant up until 1906, when the current stone structure was built. The plant still operates today, although it uses much more modern and efficient equipment.

Telluride

There is evidence that the Ute Indians, who occupied many mountain valleys of Colorado, used the area where the town of Telluride now exists as a summer camp. When miners first settled the area in the 1870s, they called the town Columbia. Because of some

LAUNDRY

Telluride's main street circa 1890. Ballard and Wasatch Mountains are visible in the distance.

confusion with Columbia, California, they renamed the town Telluride in 1878. Telluride may be named for tellurium, a mineral often associated with gold deposits, though ironically not found in the area. Some say that bandits who hid out in this canyon called it "To Hell You Ride."

When Otto Mears' railroad arrived in 1890, the town flourished and became a melting pot for many ethnic groups. Telluride's population grew to around 5,000, but in 1893 the silver crash reduced it to just a few hundred.

In the late 1970s, Telluride, like Aspen, reinvented itself. The Telluride Ski Resort opened in 1973, and the community experienced a dramatic transformation. Cultural events, festivals, music, and performing arts events now draw thousands to the town year-round. The town was designated a National Historic Landmark District in 1964. This designation helps the citizens to preserve Telluride's historically significant architecture and small-town mountain atmosphere.

Fall color frames 14,017-foot Wilson Peak, just south of Telluride.

Red Mountain Pass

View down the north side of Red Mountain Pass.

Brown Mountain
13,339 feet
Abrams Mountain
12,801 feet
Red Mountain #2
12,219 feet
Red Mountain #3
12,890 feet
US 550
N
E
106°

The most intimidating paved Colorado highway may well be that on the north side of **Red Mountain Pass.** This section of US 550 is narrow and has tight curves, precipitous drops, and few guardrails. The shoulder drops 300 feet straight down into the Uncompahgre Gorge, cut through by the Uncompahgre River. It is spectacular! The mountain views and the rich mining history of the area make it one of the "must sees" of Colorado. Ouray, at the base of the pass, is appropriately called the "Gem of the Rockies" and the "Switzerland of America." The road that crosses the pass connects the towns of Ouray and Silverton.

The topographic maps of the area show *three* Red Mountains, named 1, 2, and 3. Red Mountain Number 1 is not visible from the summit of the pass, but the other two are. Oxidized iron creates the red-orange color of these peaks, which present stunning photo opportunities, particularly at sunset.

Iron oxides create Red Mountain #2s colors, enhanced here by the glow of the setting sun.

ORIGIN OF NAME	Three peaks east of the pass are a distinctive red color and are named Red Mountain 1, 2, and 3.
ELEVATION	11,018 feet
NEARBY CITIES	Ouray/Silverton
POINTS OF INTEREST	Red Mountain, Silverton, Ouray, the Million Dollar Highway.
COUNTY	Ouray
HIGHWAY	US 550/ San Juan Skyway
MILEPOST	80.1
GPS	37°53'56"N by 107°42'43"W
TOPO MAP	Ironton
GETTING THERE	**From Ouray,** head south on US 550 for 13 miles. **From Silverton,** head northwest on US 550 for 11 miles.

The Red Mountain Mining District

Prospectors first entered the Red Mountain area in September 1879. In 1883 they established a mining town on the north side of Red Mountain Pass, naming it Ironton.

The Red Mountain Mining District covers both the north and south sides of Red Mountain Pass. In the 1880s it was one of the most prolific districts of the area, boasting nearly forty mines known worldwide for their silver production. This district produced $30 million worth of silver, lead, zinc, copper, and gold. At today's prices, that would amount to $250 million. The Yankee Girl and Guston Mines, both discovered in 1881, were two of the richest mines in the area.

Above: Colorado Boy Mine. Right: This wagon road near Red Mountain Pass was once used to transport ore and supplies between mines and local communities and railroad lines.

Right: Old house at the townsite of Ironton. Below: Mountain King Mine. Far right: Mining car rails from the Mountain King Mine. Below right: Remains of the Silver Ledge Mill, built in the early 1900s.

Above: The Silver Ledge Mine in the 1920s. Right: The abandoned mine in 2007.

The Million Dollar Highway

Before the railroad reached Ironton, most travelers going south from Ouray used Otto Mears' toll road. Mears took over the road from the Ouray and San Juan Wagon Road Company on April 1, 1880. Using techniques learned in other road construction projects, he completed it in 1884. Pack trains of mules and burros used this road

to move all the supplies the town of Ironton needed and carry out the ore from the nearby mines. It was not easy. Travel on the road was tough because of steep grades, sharp curves, narrow trails, precipitous drops, and a rough roadbed.

With the advent of automobile travel in the 1920s, the 12 miles of Mears' toll road that ran south of Ouray through the Uncompahgre Gorge became part of the "Million Dollar Highway" at great redesign costs. Cutting the road into the cliffs of the Uncompahgre Gorge was no easy task, and the project was very expensive. This part of the highway has changed little since its completion in 1924!

Tollgate on Otto Mears's Million Dollar Highway over Red Mountain Pass in the late 1800s. Photo by William Henry Jackson.

Where did Colorado State Highway 550 get the name the Million Dollar Highway?

No one really seems to know, so take your pick!

- The route includes five mountain passes, which offer a million dollars worth of scenery.
- Upgrading the road to accommodate vehicles cost $40,000 per mile, for a grand total of more than a million dollars.
- Many who traveled the highway earned million-dollar fortunes in the area.
- Mines in the area produced over $750 million in ore.
- Tailings from the mines, containing a million dollars worth of gold ore, were used for construction of the road.
- Some people say they wouldn't go back over that road for a million dollars.

Ouray

North of Ridgway at the northern base of Red Mountain Pass is the town of Ouray. Mount Abrams, to the south, and the Amphitheater formation, to the east, tower 5,000 feet over the town. Unlike many mining camps, Ouray never experienced a large fire. Because of that, it has many well-preserved, historic structures, including hotels, opera houses, and a courthouse.

Most believe that prospectors first arrived in the valley in 1875, traveling from Silverton to the south. Ouray incorporated a year later, and by1880 more than 2,500 people lived there. In 1887 the Denver & Rio Grande Railway completed a line to Ouray and opened a depot there the following year.

A narrow gauge railroad excursion came to Ouray in the same year, allowing the Denver & Rio Grande Railroad to promote its "Around the Circle" tours. The route traveled from Pueblo to Salida, then over Marshall Pass to Gunnison. It then continued to Montrose and turned south into Ouray. From there, travelers rode stagecoaches

A panorama of the town of Ouray.

up the Uncompahgre Gorge along the route of Mears' toll road to Chattanooga at the base of Red Mountain Pass. They then rode the Silverton Railroad to Silverton. In Silverton, they changed trains and rail lines to ride the Rio Grande to Durango and continue over La Veta Pass to Pueblo. These tours became very popular over the years.

Molas Pass

Molas Lake can be seen near the center of this 270-degree view of Molas Pass.

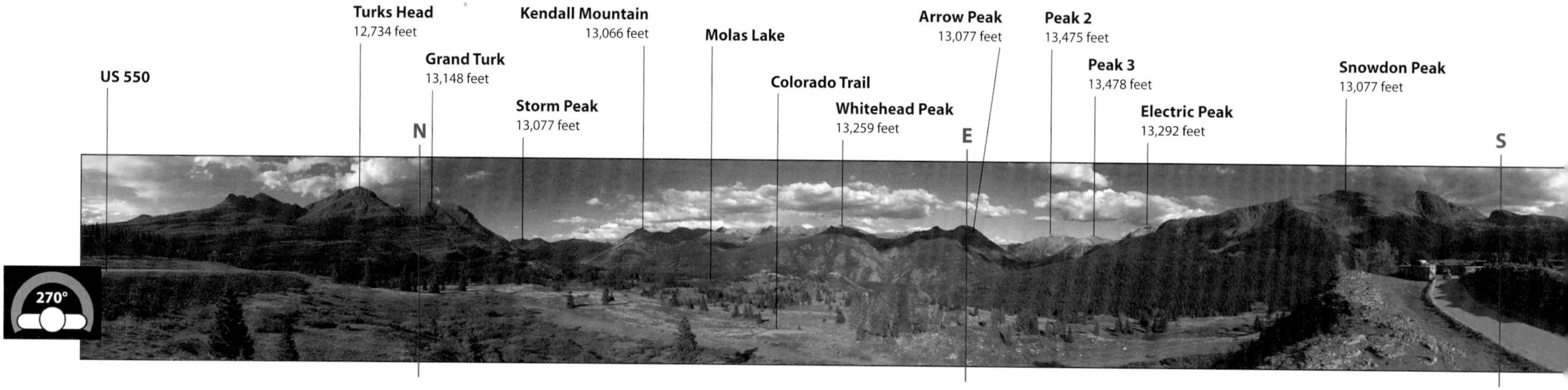
Turks Head
12,734 feet
Kendall Mountain
13,066 feet
Molas Lake
Arrow Peak
13,077 feet
Peak 2
13,475 feet
Grand Turk
13,148 feet
Peak 3
13,478 feet
Snowdon Peak
13,077 feet
US 550
Colorado Trail
Storm Peak
13,077 feet
Whitehead Peak
13,259 feet
Electric Peak
13,292 feet
N
E
S
270°

Some of the clearest air in the United States makes the view at 10,910-foot **Molas Pass** exceptional. There are days when so few visibility-reducing chemicals and particles are in the air that you can see for more than 170 miles. Many San Juan peaks towering over 13,000 feet pierce the skyline.

Where US 550 crosses Molas Pass, it is also designated as the San Juan Skyway Scenic Byway and the Million Dollar Highway. The Colorado Trail crosses the road just north of the pass. The Animas River Gorge, the route of the Durango & Silverton Narrow Gauge Railroad (D&SNGRR) lies hidden to the east, and Coal

Bank Pass is located about 7 miles southwest on US 550. Silverton lies 7 miles to the south.

Looking out across some of the areas near Molas Pass, you would think you were above timberline. In reality this was once a heavily forested area called Lime Creek. In 1879, a fire ravaged the area. Even though many community groups have planted thousands of trees since then, little of the 26,000-acre forest has returned yet, due to the high elevation and resultant slow growth of the trees.

Geology

Many geologic forces have formed the view from Molas Pass. Shallow oceans once covered this area of Colorado, leaving behind sediments. The shoreline fluctuated, and layers of silt, sand, and limestone formed the benches of the Hermosa Formation to the west.

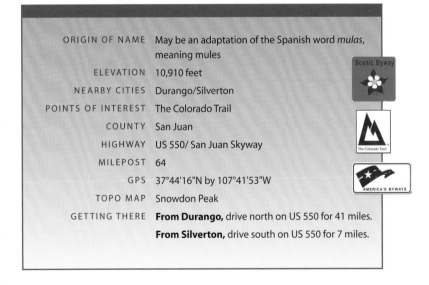

ORIGIN OF NAME	May be an adaptation of the Spanish word *mulas*, meaning mules
ELEVATION	10,910 feet
NEARBY CITIES	Durango/Silverton
POINTS OF INTEREST	The Colorado Trail
COUNTY	San Juan
HIGHWAY	US 550/ San Juan Skyway
MILEPOST	64
GPS	37°44'16"N by 107°41'53"W
TOPO MAP	Snowdon Peak
GETTING THERE	**From Durango,** drive north on US 550 for 41 miles. **From Silverton,** drive south on US 550 for 7 miles.

About 70 million years ago, volcanoes in this area erupted, forming the top layer of Sultan Mountain. The 100 miles of the backbone of the San Juan Mountains have volcanic features. Cooling magma beneath the earth's surface created the deposits of lead, copper, gold, and silver that later drew miners to this area.

About 15,000 years ago, massive glaciers a half-mile thick carved the mountains and valleys of the area. They ground out U-shaped valleys and acted as giant conveyor belts, transporting and depositing ridges, called moraines, on the sides and ends of the valleys. The glaciers have melted away, but evidence of their existence is visible all around Molas Pass.

Otto Mears, Pathfinder of the San Juans

Otto Mears was born in Kurland, Russia, in 1841. He traveled to San Francisco as an orphan, sold newspapers, and worked in California's gold fields. He fought for the Union in the Civil War and served under Kit Carson in the Navajo campaigns. The Army discharged him in Las Cruces, New Mexico, prior to his move to Colorado.

Mears owned stores and a mill in Conejos and Saguache, towns in southern Colorado. Because he needed to transport his wheat over Poncha Pass to the flourmill in Nathrop and then to Leadville, he decided to improve a road north over Poncha Pass to Lake County. Former Colorado territorial governor William Gilpin met Mears and suggested that he design the grades on the road so that they would be gradual enough for a railroad to use, while initially operating it as a toll road. The route soon became very successful. In 1871, Mears sold it to the Denver & Rio Grande (D&RG) Railroad.

Otto Mears standing in front of a train on one of his lines.

With the gold and silver discoveries in the San Juan Range, another of his toll roads became a vital link to the west. Mears had seen that the railroad was headed his direction through the Royal Gorge so he capitalized on that activity. He built a new road that ran from Salida, over Marshall Pass, to Gunnison and sold that route to the D&RG. This route allowed the D&RG to be the first railroad into Gunnison and the Crested Butte mining camps.

In 1881 he built another line from the town of Ridgway to Telluride. Two years later he completed a toll road from Ouray to Ironton up the Uncompahgre Gorge and placed the toll booth at the location of Bear Creek Falls, 580 feet above the canyon floor, making it impossible for anyone to travel up the road without paying a toll. Reportedly, this road cost $1,000 a foot to build and Mears charged $5.00 for each wagon team. In 1887, he founded the Silverton

Mears's Toll Roads

Year Completed	Road Name	Length (in miles)
1873-74	Saguache–San Juan	96
1875	Antelope Springs–Lake City	25
1877	Ouray & Lake Fork	36
1878	Lake Fork and Uncompahgre	25
1879	Poncha, Marshall & Gunnison	100
1881	Dallas & San Miguel	27
1882	San Miguel & Rico	6
1882	Gunnison–Cebolla	20
1883	Ouray–San Juan	12
1883-84	Ouray & Canyon Creek	10
1884	Silverton–Red Mountain	12
1885	Sapinero–Barnum	50
1885-86	Silverton–Mineral Point	15

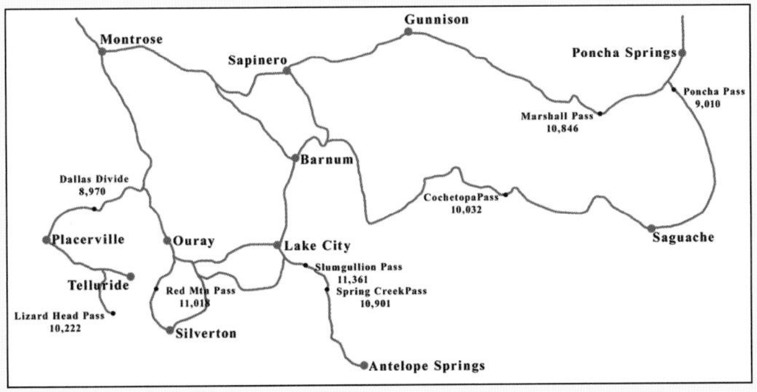
Gunnison
Montrose
Sapinero
Poncha Springs
Poncha Pass
9,010
Marshall Pass
10,846
Barnum
Dallas Divide
8,970
CochetopaPass
10,032
Placerville
Ouray
Lake City
Saguache
Telluride
Slumgullion Pass
11,361
Spring CreekPass
10,901
Lizard Head Pass
10,222
Silverton
Antelope Springs

Otto Mears's toll roads.

Railroad Company and built tracks from Silverton up Cement Creek to Red Mountain Town and Ironton, along the route of the toll road that he had previously built. Eventually the county purchased the road from Mears, transforming it into what is now US 550, the "Million Dollar Highway."

The Denver & Rio Grande Railroad hired Mears as a track builder in the San Juans. The lines he laid for them followed many of his toll roads. Otto Mears and investors in Denver also constructed a narrow gauge line, called the Rio Grande Southern Railroad, which served the western area of the San Juans. Soon Mears owned the railroads he built, eventually owning four separate lines around the Silverton area.

The Rio Grande Southern Railroad passed through the mining and lumber towns of Telluride, Ophir, Lizard Head, Rico, Dolores, and Hesperus. It reached Rico in 1891 and eliminated traffic on the Rockwood and Rico Wagon Road, finally reaching Durango from the west in 1893. The route avoided some of the more rugged terrain of the mountains and the Uncompahgre Gorge. It connected the D&RG on the north at Ridgway and on the south at Durango. The trains were mixed, meaning that they carried both freight and passengers. This route is still considered as one of the most incredible railroad lines ever built.

In 1896 the United States debated its policy about silver coinage. Maintaining silver coinage would help Mears because silver would come from his silver mines and be transported over his railroads. He traveled to the East Coast to join the debate and while there he formed the Mack Motor Company that built Mack trucks. He did return to Colorado, but later moved back to California.

Mears built nearly 450 miles of roads in the San Juans, roads that coursed through some of the most rugged and spectacular scenery in Colorado. He could truly be called an empire builder. Otto Mears was only five feet tall, but his stature had nothing to do with his drive. He died in 1931.

Coal Bank Pass

View looking east from just north of the Coal Bank Pass summit.

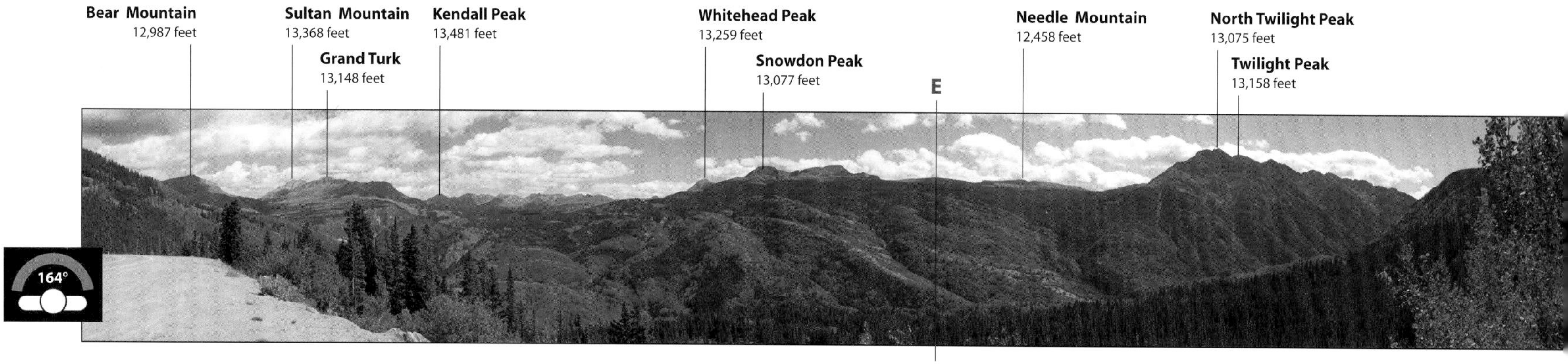
Bear Mountain
12,987 feet
Sultan Mountain
13,368 feet
Grand Turk
13,148 feet
Kendall Peak
13,481 feet
Whitehead Peak
13,259 feet
Snowdon Peak
13,077 feet
E
Needle Mountain
12,458 feet
North Twilight Peak
13,075 feet
Twilight Peak
13,158 feet
164°

Coal Bank Pass, on US 550, is part of the scenic San Juan Skyway, a 236-mile loop of paved road through the San Juan Mountains. This stretch of highway holds even more designations: it is also an All-American Road, a National Forest Scenic Byway, and a Colorado Scenic & Historic Byway.

From Durango, the road heads north and passes Boyce Lake and the Durango Mountain Resort. Pigeon and Turret Mountains, both over 13,000 feet, dominate the horizon here. Three of Colorado's fourteeners—Windom, Eolus, and Sunlight Peaks—soon come into view to the south. The road then begins the ascent to

Coal Bank Pass, where it tops out at 10,640 feet. The highway descends a short distance before beginning another climb to Molas Pass, about 7 miles northeast.

Ute Negotiations

The Ute Indians, often called "the mountain people," occupied much of Colorado for centuries. They considered the San Juan Mountains their stronghold. However, when the Territory of Colorado was created in 1861, William Gilpin, the first territorial governor, believed that the Ute should be removed from the mining areas in the San Juan Mountains and placed on reservations elsewhere in the territory. His successor, John Evans, believed the same thing.

In 1863 Governor Evans convened a meeting with the Ute in Conejos. Representatives from many Ute tribes attended. Chief

ORIGIN OF NAME	Coal can be seen in the road banks along the roadway.
ELEVATION	10,640 feet
NEARBY CITIES	Durango/Silverton
POINTS OF INTEREST	San Juan Skyway, The Durango & Silverton Narrow Gauge Railroad
COUNTY	San Juan
HIGHWAY	US 550/ San Juan Skyway
MILEPOST	56.5
GPS	37°42'02"N by 37°42'02"N
TOPO MAP	Engineer Mountain
GETTING THERE	**From Durango,** travel north on US 550 for 34 miles. **From Silverton,** travel south on US 550 for 14 miles.

Scenic Byway

AMERICA'S BYWAYS

Ouray and his wife Chipeta had worked hard to keep the peace between the whites and the Indians and convinced the Ute to agree to the treaty Evans offered, which placed the Ute on a large reservation on the Western Slope of Colorado.

By 1868 a new treaty moved the Ute to a reservation in southwestern Colorado that covered an area totaling one-third of the territory. This treaty stated that the U.S. government would provide each Ute family 160 acres of land, as well as farming tools, seeds, livestock, schools, and sawmills. As soon as it was ratified, another territorial governor, Edward M. McCook, took office. He believed the treaty was much too generous.

Utes and whites pose after signing the Brunot Agreement in 1874. Front row, left to right: Guero, Chipeta, Ouray, Piah (Ouray's brother). Second row: Uriah M. Curtis, Major J.B. Thompson, General Charles Adams, Otto Mears. Back Row: Washington, Susan (Ouray's sister), Johnson, Jack, John.

Around this same time, the secretary of the interior named Felix R. Brunot as president of the Board of Indian Commissioners. Brunot entered into negotiations with the Ute that in 1873 resulted in the Brunot Agreement, also known as the San Juan Cession. This agreement removed 4 million acres of the San Juan Mountains from the reservation system and opened up the area to settlement and mining. Article II of the agreement made this statement concerning the 4 million acres: "The United States shall permit the Ute Indians to hunt upon said lands so long as the game lasts and the Indian are at peace with the white man." The Ute reluctantly signed the treaty, but believed they were selling the mountain's peaks while the settlers believed they had bought the entire San Juans.

By 1881, most Ute had been forcibly removed from all but a small corner of southwest Colorado. The reservations they were relocated to were a considerable distance from their traditional summer hunting ranges and they experienced great difficulty surviving on the new land. Today the Ute rely heavily on revenues from oil and gas, as well as casinos, to increase their income. The Ute leaders continue to develop economic and educational opportunities for their tribes while also trying to preserve their language and traditional culture.

The Durango and Silverton Narrow Gauge Railroad

The Durango & Silverton Narrow Gauge Railroad (D&SNGRR) provides the single most important attraction in the town of Durango. The train travels north through the town to meet the Animas

River, which it follows to Silverton. The railroad line does not travel past Coal Bank Pass, but on the other side of the West Needle Mountain range to the east.

Construction of this line was completed in 1882. In its heyday, the D&SNGRR hauled hundreds of millions of dollars worth of ore from Colorado mines. However, as Colorado's Gold Rush ended and mines began closing down, use of the D&SNGRR line declined. It might have gone out of operation had Hollywood not stepped in. Authentic westerns often needed vintage trains, and the D&SNGRR fit the bill. The trains of the Durango & Silverton "starred" in the following films:

Colorado Territory (1949)
Ticket to Tomahawk (1950)
Denver & Rio Grande (1952)
Viva Zapata (1952)
Three Young Texans (1954)
Run for Cover (1955)
Maverick Queen (1956)
Around the World in 80 Days (1956)
Night Passage (1957)
How the West Was Won (1963)
Butch Cassidy and the Sundance Kid (1969)
Support Your Local Gunfighter (1970)
Durango & Silverton Narrow Gauge Railroad (1984)
The Tracker (1987)
Rebirth of a Locomotive (1992)
Tracks Through Time (1999)
Durango Kids (1999)

The remains of the Detroit Mine near the town of Silverton.

Golden Dreams (2000)
The Claim (2000).

This new visibility renewed interest in the D&SNGRR. The entire railroad was listed as a National Historic Landmark on July 4, 1961, and it was placed on the National Register of Historic Places on October 15, 1966. In addition, the entire 530 acres of the town of Silverton became a National Historic Landmark in 1961. In the 1960s the Durango & Silverton also received the honor of being named a National Historic Civil Engineering Landmark.

The Iron Horse Bicycle Classic

The Durango & Silverton Narrow Gauge Railroad (D&SNGRR) once provided transportation between Durango and Silverton for miners, ore, and tourists. Listed as a National Historic Landmark in 1961, the train still runs, carrying tourists along a steep, scenic climb. It does not climb over Coal Bank Pass, but rather runs east of it, along the Needle Mountain Range.

A locomotive belches smoke on its journey between Durango and Silverton.

The Iron Horse Bicycle Classic originated in 1972 from a crazy idea. Why not race the train from Durango to Silverton on a bike? Jim Mayer, a brakeman on the D&SNGRR, and his brother, Tom, decided to formalize the challenge.

Tom left Durango (6,512 feet) at the same time as the train and peddled up to Coal Bank Pass (10,640 feet) before dropping down to Lime Creek (9,652 feet). After another climb to the top of Molas Pass (10,910 feet) he headed down to Silverton (9,305 feet), where he waited for his brother to arrive by train.

Today more than a thousand cyclists challenge the train in The Iron Horse Bicycle Classic. Since 1994, the highway over the two high mountain passes has been closed to automobile traffic during the event because of the high number of riders. Professionals complete the 50-mile road race with a 5,700-foot vertical gain in around two hours.

The D&SNGRR Today

This historic train, in continuous operation since it was built, is now a scenic, tourist railroad. It still uses vintage steam locomotives to pull refurbished rolling stock consistent with what was originally used on the line. The locomotives, also maintained in their original condition, are coal-fired and steam-operated. The line's inventory includes seven active locomotives, three diesel locomotives, and three locomotives in static displays. Its rolling stock includes 49 passenger cars, open gondolas, concessions, private cars, and boxcars, and cabooses.

Hundreds of miles of narrow gauge track were once laid across Colorado. Opposite: The D&SNGRR still uses locomotives and passenger cars that were built between the 1880s and 1920s.

486
DURANGO

The D&SNGRR traverses the highline above the Animas River.

The train requires only four employees to operate: an engineer, a fireman, a brakeman, and a conductor. The conductor is in charge of the train, and the brakeman assists the conductor. The fireman shovels six tons of coal on a roundtrip, and during that time the boiler uses ten thousand gallons of water. The engineer operates the controls of the locomotive under the direction of the conductor. Both the fireman and the engineer carefully watch the water level in the boiler. If the water level were to drop below a critical level, a devastating boiler explosion could result. A concessions staff and private car attendants provide the creature comforts for passengers on the train.

A ride on the Durango & Silverton Railroad is a treat for the senses. Some describe the train as a coal-fueled, steam-powered time machine. With the sights, sounds, and smells of the train, it is easy

to imagine what the tourists in the late 1800s experienced when enjoying the only form of transportation that did not require bone jarring hard work or one's ability to hang on for dear life.

Above: Passengers in Silverton prepare to board a D&SNGRR train that has turned around and is ready to return to Durango. Top: This restored coach car accommodates those who do not wish to be exposed to the elements.

Top: Riding in open observation car, or gondola, is the best way to enjoy the sights, sounds, and smells of the D&SNGRR. Above: In the town of Silverton, crews turn the trains in the wye.

The D&SNGRR operates daily from the first of May to the end of October, carrying around a quarter of a million passengers a year. Many also enjoy a winter excursion to Cascade Canyon.

The D&SNGRR maintains two museums. One is in Durango at the south end of the roundhouse. The other is in the Silverton Freight Yard in the Silverton Depot. Admission for both is included in the train ticket and is good for two days prior to or two days following the ride on the train.

DURANGO & SILVERTON
473

Top: The parlor car is reserved for special guests. Above: A locomotive equipped with a snowplow heads towards Silverton along the highline.

Slumgullion Pass

View looking west from just west of the summit of Slumgullion Pass at the Windy Point Overlook.

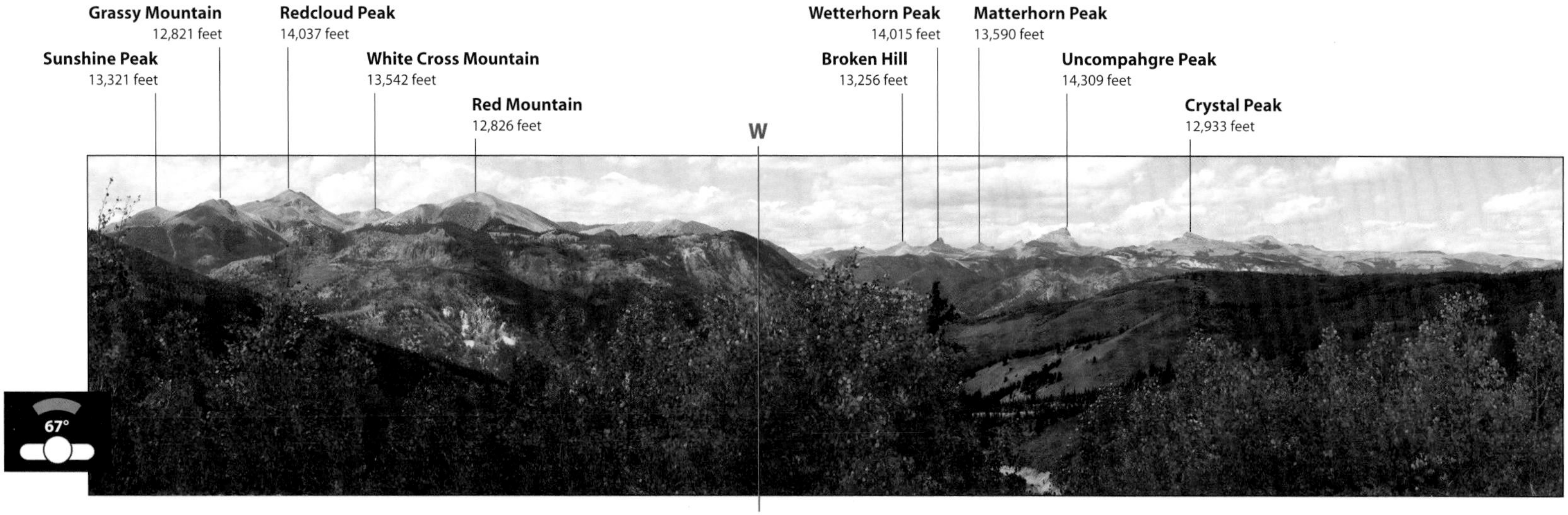
Grassy Mountain
12,821 feet
Sunshine Peak
13,321 feet
Redcloud Peak
14,037 feet
White Cross Mountain
13,542 feet
Red Mountain
12,826 feet
W
Wetterhorn Peak
14,015 feet
Broken Hill
13,256 feet
Matterhorn Peak
13,590 feet
Uncompahgre Peak
14,309 feet
Crystal Peak
12,933 feet
67°

Fourteener Uncompahgre Peak is one of Colorado's highest at 14,309 feet.

Slumgullion Pass crests at an altitude of 11,361 feet and is located on Colorado Highway 149, the Silver Thread Scenic Byway, between Creede and Lake City. Windy Point Overlook, approximately 1 mile west of the pass, offers views of numerous peaks that are above 13,000 feet, including the impressive 14,309-foot Uncompahgre Peak.

In the 1870s, Henry Finley, President of the Lake City Town Company, led the construction of a road over Slumgullion Pass. This 81-mile road connecting Lake City to Creede reduced the average travel time between the then-mining camps from three days to a day

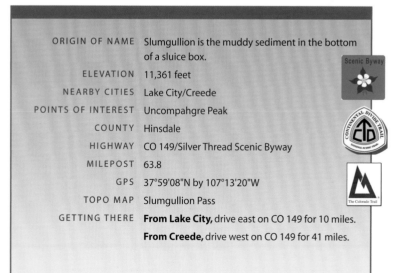

ORIGIN OF NAME	Slumgullion is the muddy sediment in the bottom of a sluice box.
ELEVATION	11,361 feet
NEARBY CITIES	Lake City/Creede
POINTS OF INTEREST	Uncompahgre Peak
COUNTY	Hinsdale
HIGHWAY	CO 149/Silver Thread Scenic Byway
MILEPOST	63.8
GPS	37°59'08"N by 107°13'20"W
TOPO MAP	Slumgullion Pass
GETTING THERE	**From Lake City,** drive east on CO 149 for 10 miles. **From Creede,** drive west on CO 149 for 41 miles.

Lake San Cristobal, Colorado's second largest natural lake after Grand Lake.

and a half. Very steep sections of the road were "corduroyed"—laid with logs 6 to 12 inches in diameter—to reduce erosion. It made for a very interesting ride in a stagecoach.

Slumgullion Mudslide

Most visible geologic features in Colorado are thousands to millions of years old. Not so with the Slumgullion earthflow, or mudslide. Around 700 years ago, volcanic tuff and breccia on the south slope of Mesa Seco became saturated with heavy rain. The material broke loose and oozed its way down the mountain, descending 3,000 feet and traveling more than 4 miles. The flow dammed up the Lake Fork of the Gunnison River and created Lake San Cristobal, Colorado's second largest natural lake.

Left: North Clear Creek Falls east of Spring Creek Pass. Above: View east from the summit of Spring Creek Pass.

Slumgullion Stew

- 1½ lb. stew meat
- 1 sliced onion
- 1 bunch carrots
- 3 red potatoes
- 1 bell pepper
- 1 can black-eyed peas
- 1 can tomatoes
- 4–6 cups water
- leftover cabbage, corn, green beans, etc.
- salt, pepper, and thyme to taste.
- flour
- ½ cup of macaroni

Combine all ingredients except macaroni in a large pot. Add flour to desired consistency. Simmer over low heat until the vegetables are almost soft. Add macaroni and cook for ½ hour.

A second flow began about 350 years ago and is still moving at a rate of about twenty feet per year. Tilted trees in the mudflow are evidence of the slide's active state.

The name "Slumgullion Pass" came about because the color of the sliding mud reminded local gold miners of the muddy sediments, called slumgullion, in their sluice boxes. Miners also made a colorful stew that they called slumgullion.

Alferd Packer—The San Juan Cannibal

Mystery, tall tales, and unconfirmed rumors surround the story of Alferd Packer, sometimes called "The San Juan Cannibal." In 1883, Packer was tried for and convicted of manslaughter in Lake City after reputably eating five of his prospecting companions while snowbound near Slumgullion Pass.

Right: It is obvious from the tree growth that the Slumgullion Mudslide is still active.
Opposite: The Slumgullion Mudslide stands out in this view from the roadway near the Lake San Cristobal Overlook.

Monument at the site of the massacre at the base of Slumgullion Pass.

Packer migrated to Colorado from Pennsylvania in 1862 at the age of twenty. In 1873, he was hired as a guide by some men from Salt Lake City for a prospecting trip into the Lake City area. Some reports say that he knew very little about the area. In January the party attempted a mountain crossing against the advice of many and were reported lost.

When Packer showed up at the Los Pinos Indian Agency four months later looking none the worse for wear, some became suspicious. He appeared well fed and had a lot of money with him. His explanation as to what happened to him and the rest of the party changed with every telling. In one popular version, Packer said he came back from a scouting mission to find that one of his companions had gone berserk, killing the others and roasting their flesh over a fire. He said that he then shot him in self-defense.

An Indian guide later reported that he found strips of human flesh on the trail where Packer was, and in August of 1894 the camp of the five missing men was found near Slumgullion Pass, 2 miles from Lake City. Packer was arrested, but escaped. He lived in Wyoming for nine years under an assumed name until he was recaptured and returned to Lake City to be tried. He was found guilty of murder and sentenced to be hanged.

One story reports that Judge Melville B. Gerry, on pronouncing sentencing, said: "There was siven Dimmycrats in Hinsdale County! But you, yah voracious, man-eatin son of a bitch, yah et five

THIS TABLET ERECTED
IN MEMORY OF
ISRAEL SWAN
GEORGE NOON
FRANK MILLER
JAMES HUMPHREYS
WILSON BELL
WHO WERE MURDERED ON THIS SPOT
EARLY IN THE YEAR 1874
WHILE PIONEERING
THE MINERAL RESOURCES
OF THE SAN JUAN COUNTRY

Tablet erected in the memory of the men who were murdered near Slumgullion Pass.

of them, therefor I sentence ye t' be hanged by the neck until y're dead, dead, dead!"

The verdict was later reduced to manslaughter and Packer was sentenced to forty years in prison. He was paroled in January 1901. Six years later, Packer died of natural causes and was buried at Littleton's Prince Avenue Cemetery near Denver.

Years after Packer's death, the citizens of Lake City built a monument at the site of the massacre. The inscription on the marker reads: "This tablet erected in memory of Israel Swan, George Noon, Frank Miller, James Humphreys, Wilson Bell, who were murdered on this spot early in the year 1874 while pioneering the mineral resources of the San Juan Country."

There are still many unknowns regarding what happened to the Packer party. In July of 1989, photographers and local media were on hand when a team of anthropologists and archaeologists exhumed the bones of the murdered men. Some of the bodies had blunt force blows to the head and cuts to the arms and hands. Nicks on some of the bones may have been made by a knife. Not everyone supports the findings, but many say they show that Packer did indeed kill and cannibalize the men. After the investigation, the remains were reburied in a wooden box on the site.

Wolf Creek Pass

Views from the Lobo Overlook above Wolf Creek Pass, looking toward the Wolf Creek Pass ski area.

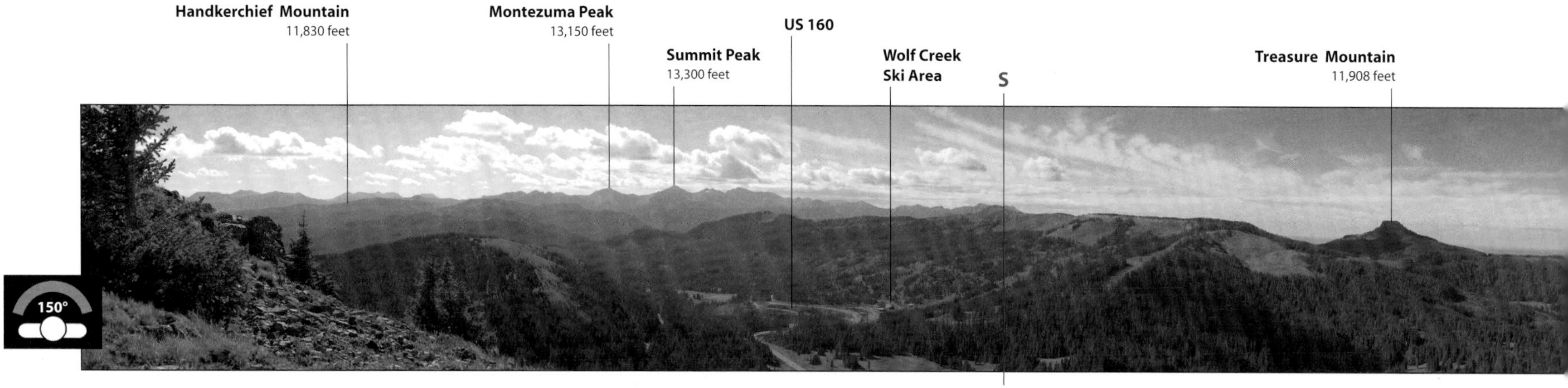
Handkerchief Mountain
11,830 feet
Montezuma Peak
13,150 feet
Summit Peak
13,300 feet
US 160
Wolf Creek
Ski Area
S
Treasure Mountain
11,908 feet
150°

In the heart of the San Juan Mountains, 24 miles east of Pagosa Springs on US 160, is one of the more famous passes in Colorado, **Wolf Creek Pass**. This pass is home to Wolf Creek Ski Area and the namesake of country singer C.W. McCall's hit song "Wolf Creek Pass." There is a large parking lot on the 10,850-foot summit.

The pass is on the Continental Divide and separates two well-known rivers. On the west of the pass is the San Juan River, a major tributary of the Colorado River, which drains into the Pacific Ocean. On the east side of the pass is the Rio Grande, which drains into the Atlantic.

While the local demands of lumber and mining camps prompted the construction of many mountain roads in Colorado, the one over

ORIGIN OF NAME	Named for a trapper, Bill Wolf.
ELEVATION	10,850 feet
NEARBY CITIES	Pagosa Springs/Del Norte
POINTS OF INTEREST	Continental Divide, Lobo Overlook, Wolf Creek Ski Area, Weminuche Wilderness, and Treasure Falls
COUNTY	Mineral
HIGHWAY	US 160
MILEPOST	166.8
GPS	37°28'57"N by 106°47'56"W
TOPO MAP	Wolf Creek Pass
GETTING THERE	**From Pagosa Springs,** travel east on US 160 for 23 miles. **From Del Norte,** travel west on US 160 for 35 miles.

Cumbres Pass was built to facilitate transcontinental travel. Some documents indicate that the pass was first completed in 1913, others 1916.

Lobo Overlook

At the summit of Wolf Creek Pass there is a turnoff for a well-graded, 3-mile dirt road that travels north to the top of a hill called the Lobo Overlook. You can enjoy 360-degree views from this vantage point, and the short detour is well worth the time. There is also a parking area here and a trailhead for the Continental Divide Trail.

Weminuche Wilderness

From Lobo Overlook, above Wolf Creek Pass, you can see a portion of the Weminuche Wilderness Area. Located in the San Juan and Rio Grande National Forests, this 492,418-acre wilderness area is by far Colorado's largest.

Early tourists pose by their car and a sign that reads:"Wolf Creek Pass—Elevation 10,800 Ft."

Looking east from the Lobo Overlook above Wolf Creek Pass.

Weminuche is at the heart of the San Juan mountain range, and has an average elevation of over 10,000 feet, and many of its peaks rise over 13,000 feet. In the far western side of the Weminuche, where it crosses into the Needle Mountains, there are three 14,000-foot peaks: Sunlight Peak, Windom Peak, and Mount Eolus.

Dozens of major streams and rivers travel through the Weminuche on their way to feed the Rio Grande and San Juan Rivers. There are also 63 lakes in this area.

Nearly 500 miles of trail cross the Weminuche. The Continental Divide Trail runs through the area for nearly 80 miles. The Colorado Trail crosses it for 21 miles, running from Molas Pass to the Rio Grande.

La Garita Volcano

Looking out to the northwest from the Lobo Overlook, you can see the La Garita Mountains, formed by La Garita Volcano's first eruption 27.8 million years ago. This massive volcanic event makes

Mount St. Helens' famous 1980 eruption look like a soap bubble pop. It is believed that in less than a week, 3,000 cubic miles of magma flowed from La Garita. That is enough to bury the state of Colorado under 61 feet of magma! This magma, called tuff, makes up the surrounding La Garita Mountains to the north. The eruption most likely killed everything from the nearby La Garita Mountains all the way east into what is now Kansas. Some of the ash would have fallen as far as the East Coast. The scale of this eruption is far beyond anything known in human history.

When La Garita erupted, it formed one of the world's largest calderas. A caldera is a large depression formed when the magma chamber below a volcano is emptied during an eruption and the mountain collapses into the chamber. Most calderas are circular, but the La Garita caldera is an oval that is 22 miles wide and 50 miles long. Because the La Garita formation is so large, has an unusual shape, and has been changed in form by erosion, additional volcanism, and glaciations, it was not discovered until 1995.

Wolf Creek Ski Area

Just east of the summit of Wolf Creek Pass is the Wolf Creek Ski Area. Skiers have frequented this area since the 1930s. Before there were lifts, they would park at the summit of the pass, then hike up and ski down the hills around it. In the fall of 1938, the forest service and the Civilian Conservation Corp (CCC) constructed a shelter house for skiers on the summit of the pass. Local papers from that time reported that there were often fifty automobiles parked on top of the pass.

In 1955, the Wolf Creek Ski Development Corporation constructed facilities at their present location. Wolf Creek Ski Area can rightfully claim to have "The Most Snow in Colorado"—their average snowfall is more than 38 feet!

Country Music and a Truckload of Chickens

The road west from the summit goes down a very steep grade, and though it is a well paved, and mostly four-laned, it has a reputation

View of the Weminuche Wilderness from the Lobo Overlook.

> **Runaway Truck!**
>
> Wherever possible, the steep sections of many mountain passes in Colorado have runaway truck ramps that can be used by truckers who lose their breaks. These ramps are designed to allow truckers to exit the roadway and slow down their vehicle quickly and safely. They are built up hillsides and covered with heavy gravel. The gravel is so deep that a truck that uses a ramp must be towed back down to the roadway. You can see one of these ramps when descending the west side of Wolf Creek Pass.

among truckers for being difficult and dangerous. Country singer C. W. McCall's song "Wolf Creek Pass," released in 1975, greatly enhanced this reputation.

The song tells a story of two truckers who are hauling chickens. On their way down the west side of the pass, they lose control of their 18-wheeler. After a harrowing ride, they bash into the side of the feed store in downtown Pagosa Springs. The early part of the song's description is entirely possible, but the crash into the feed store is not so likely. The out-of-control truck would have to successfully negotiate the switchback curves coming down from the pass, then coast the long, level road into Pagosa Springs before crashing into the store.

The story does, however, draw attention to the risks that trucks face when crossing the passes of Colorado. Safety for travelers on mountain highways is important to the Colorado Department of Transportation (CDOT). Trucks are required to use low gears and

travel at slow speeds to prevent brake failures. Runaway truck ramps are built into especially steep sections of highway, should failure occur, and many highways have very sturdy guardrails to prevent vehicles from leaving the roadway.

Death at Wagon Wheel Gap

John Frémont and his party passed through this area on their ill-fated expedition to find a route for the transcontinental railroad through the San Juan Mountains. When the party attempted to abandon the expedition by heading back to the Front Range, ten feet of snow stopped their progress somewhere near the town of Wagon Wheel Gap, on the east side of Wolf Creek Pass. Ten of Frémont's men died of cold and starvation.

Cumbres Pass

View from Cumbres Pass, with a Cumbres and Toltec Scenic Railroad doubleheader coming up the pass from the west.

Eastbound
C&TSRR
SE
S
SW
W
173°

Cumbres Pass is located 12.5 miles east of Chama, New Mexico, and 36 miles west of Antonito, Colorado, on CO 17. It is Colorado's most southern pass, and also one of its warmest. This does not mean that the area is without snow! The average yearly snowfall on Cumbres Pass is 22 feet. In 1957, two trains carrying fifty-eight men were stranded on the pass for seven days because of a large snowstorm.

Trains still run over the pass, and a rail yard for the Cumbres and Toltec Scenic Railroad (C&TSRR) sits at the summit. This rail yard is a living museum. A number of its buildings, including a train depot and a section house, are the restored remains of a small town named Alta.

ORIGIN OF NAME	*Cumbres* is Spanish for summit, peak, or crest.
ELEVATION	10,022 feet
NEARBY CITIES	Chama, NM/Antonito, CO
POINTS OF INTEREST	Cumbres and Toltec Scenic Railroad
COUNTY	Conejos
HIGHWAY	CO 17/ Los Caminos Antiguos
MILEPOST	64
GPS	37°01'14"N by 106°27'00"W
TOPO MAP	Cumbres
GETTING THERE	**From Chama, NM,** travel east on NM 17 for 12 miles, crossing into Colorado. **From Antonito,** travel west on CO 17 for 36 miles.

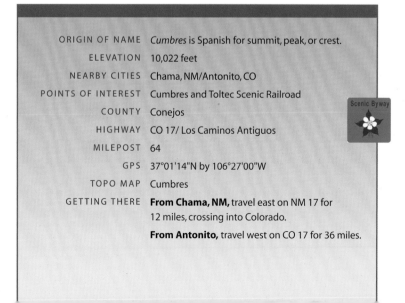

Scenic Byway

488
488
Cumbres & Toltec

A locomotive at the summit town of Alta.

The history of Cumbres Pass goes back to long before there were railroads. Archeological findings indicate that people have inhabited this area for 11,000 years. The 10,022-foot summit of the pass is the high point for a Scenic and Historic Byway called Los Caminos Antiguos, or "The Ancient Roads."

Wagons first began crossing Cumbres Pass in 1876. The journey was both dangerous and difficult. Many wagons had no brakes, so trees were dragged behind them when descending steep hillsides. If the route was extremely steep, it was sometimes necessary to lower the wagons using ropes. In 1880, the Denver & Rio Grande Railroad extended their line over Cumbres Pass.

Little evidence of civilization enters the view from Cumbres Pass except for the C&TSRR rail yard and some homes and cabins a few miles east of the summit. The Rio Grande National Forest encompasses most of the surrounding land. Its open meadows and fertile valleys join together to create spectacular scenery.

The Cumbres and Toltec Scenic Railroad

The Cumbres and Toltec Scenic Railroad (C&TSRR) is a living museum—a fully operational railroad that allows visitors to enjoy the smoke, whistles, and chugs of the now-rare narrow gauge locomotives. Paid professional railroaders operate the equipment, but volunteers for Friends of the Cumbres & Toltec Scenic Railroad work

Left: Sunflowers line the roadway in August. Above: A locomotive fit with a snowplow, a vital piece of equipment for trains in the 1880s.

484
Cumbres & Toltec

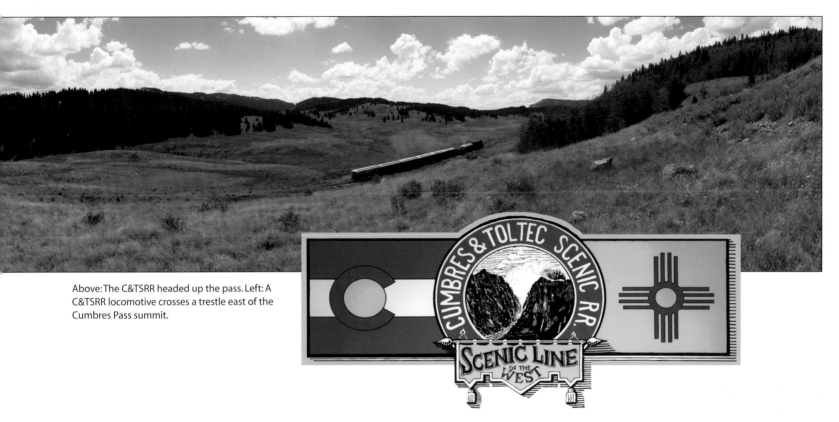

Above: The C&TSRR headed up the pass. Left: A C&TSRR locomotive crosses a trestle east of the Cumbres Pass summit.

on restoration and preservation of the structures and equipment. Thousands of tourists enjoy riding this railroad every year.

The C&TSRR is the only operational railroad in Colorado that crosses a pass. It is also America's highest and longest narrow gauge railroad, covering 64 winding miles of exposed terrain and stunning views. It is the last operational section of the Denver & Rio Grande Railroad.

The Denver & Rio Grande Railroad dismantled a huge amount of track along this line before 1970, when the states of New Mexico and Colorado purchased the remaining track, nine steam locomotives, 130 cars, all rail structures along this section, and the Chama yard. For $547,120 the C&TSRR became a reality. It began transporting tourists the following summer. Without the efforts of many railroad enthusiasts, this section might well have met the same fate as most of Colorado's narrow gauge rails!

New Mexico and Colorado cooperate to maintain this line through the Cumbres & Toltec Scenic Railroad Commission, an interstate agency authorized by an act of Congress in 1974. Today the Friends of the Cumbres & Toltec Scenic Railroad, a nonprofit, member-based organization, help to preserve and interpret the history of the railroad.

Above: A double-header pulls a passenger train of tourists up the C&TSRR. Right: An eastbound train belches smoke as it ascends the grade coming out of Chama, New Mexico. Opposite: Coordination is vital to running a double-header configuration.

Making the Grade

A train ascending the west side of Cumbres Pass has a challenge. Between Chama and the summit of Cumbres pass, they gain 2,159 feet in elevation. The grade is very steep, rising 4 vertical feet for every 100 feet of track.

In order to get up the mountain at a reasonable speed, the operators use a procedure called "double heading." This involves attaching two locomotives to the front of the train and requires a great deal of coordination between the engineers driving them.

At some points it is necessary for one of the locomotives to disengage before the train crosses a trestle, since the weight of both of them together could damage it. The first travels over the trestle by itself. Then the second pulls the rest of the train over. When the entire train is on the other side, the first locomotive is reconnected and the train proceeds on up the line. At the summit of Cumbres pass, one locomotive is disconnected and returns to Chama. The second can now handle the remainder of the trip.

Cumbres & Toltec
488
Cumbres & Toltec
484

Notes on Photographing Mountain Passes

Each panoramic image in this book is constructed of a series of many digital images "stitched" together in Adobe Photoshop. Most of the photographs capture a scope of vision of around 90 degrees, while some include a full circle, 360 degrees. Finding a high vantage point to shoot from, such as a cliff or a steep hillside, was necessary to achieve this scope.

I shot most of the images in this book on a 6.3 megapixel Canon EOS Digital Rebel SLR camera with a standard EF-S 18-55mm F/3.5-5.6 zoom lens. Don't use a wide-angle lens to shoot for panoramas, as your images will have a distorted "bow tie" or "barrel" appearance, particularly at the top and bottom of the scene. This makes merging the images difficult. Special wide-angle rectilinear lenses can reduce the distortion.

A special tripod mount designed for shooting panoramas.

Shoot in RAW format to maintain the highest image quality. Using a small aperture—f16 or smaller—is necessary to achieve proper depth of field. The exposure and focus must be the same for all segments so that the margins where the photos were merged do not vary. For this reason, set your exposure manually. You need to focus manually as well. I chose not to use any lens filters, since they often alter exposure on the edges of the photograph.

Shoot from a tripod, but not with the camera mounted to the tripod socket, which may cause parallax problems with objects in the foreground. Instead, the camera must rotate around the nodal point of the lens, the virtual center of the lens. A special mount I designed places the camera with the nodal point of the lens above the axis of the tripod head. This hardware rotates the camera around the center of the lens in such a way that there is no parallax problem when merging the images for the panorama.

Setting up the camera for the shot requires a great deal of care. The camera must be "square" on its tripod. A slight variation makes it difficult to create the panorama. Glue a bubble level to the tripod head. When the tripod is set up, adjust its legs so that the center axis of the tripod head is absolutely perpendicular. Level the head of the tripod so that it is at a right angle to the axis.

As you are taking the photos, rotate the camera so that each image overlaps the adjacent image by about 1/16th to 1/8th of the total image area. This overlap allows the images to be easily combined using Photoshop. Larger overlaps will usually create a better merge. When taking the photos, use a remote shutter release to minimize any camera shake. Don't allow the camera to rise or drop as you rotate it, or you'll create a panorama with a slope or swing.

The series of photos must be shot quickly, especially if there are clouds, which may move during the time it takes to rotate the camera. Moving clouds can impact the panorama not only by the area of the sky they cover, but also by the shadows that they cast on the scene. It is also important to consider cars, people, and any other moving object that could end up in more than one image in the scene. If an object is in the margin of one photo and not in the margin of the photo it overlaps, the merged photos do not blend well.

I recommend taking panoramic photos mid-day. The lighting when the sun is high is more consistent across the scene. In the ideal

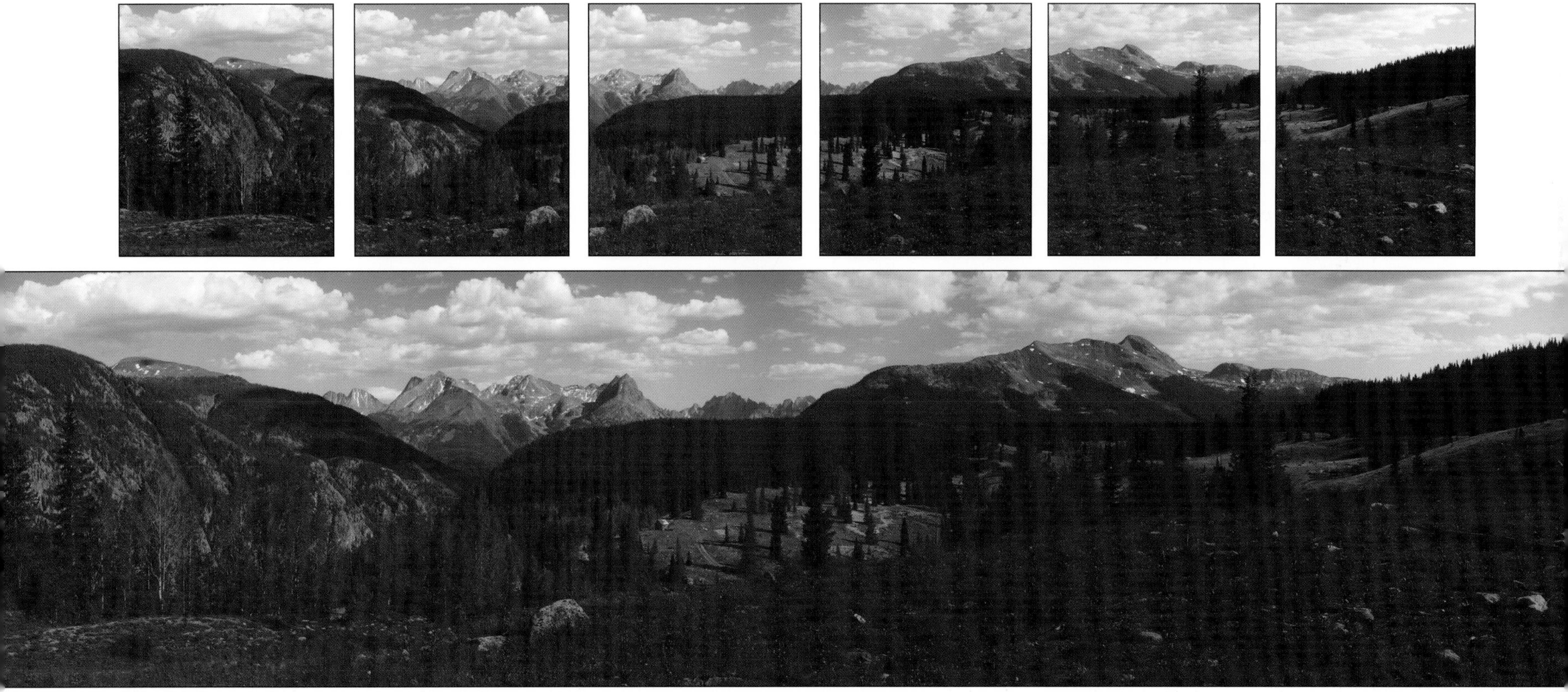

These individual images were combined to create a panorama of Molas Pass. Notice that the images overlap.

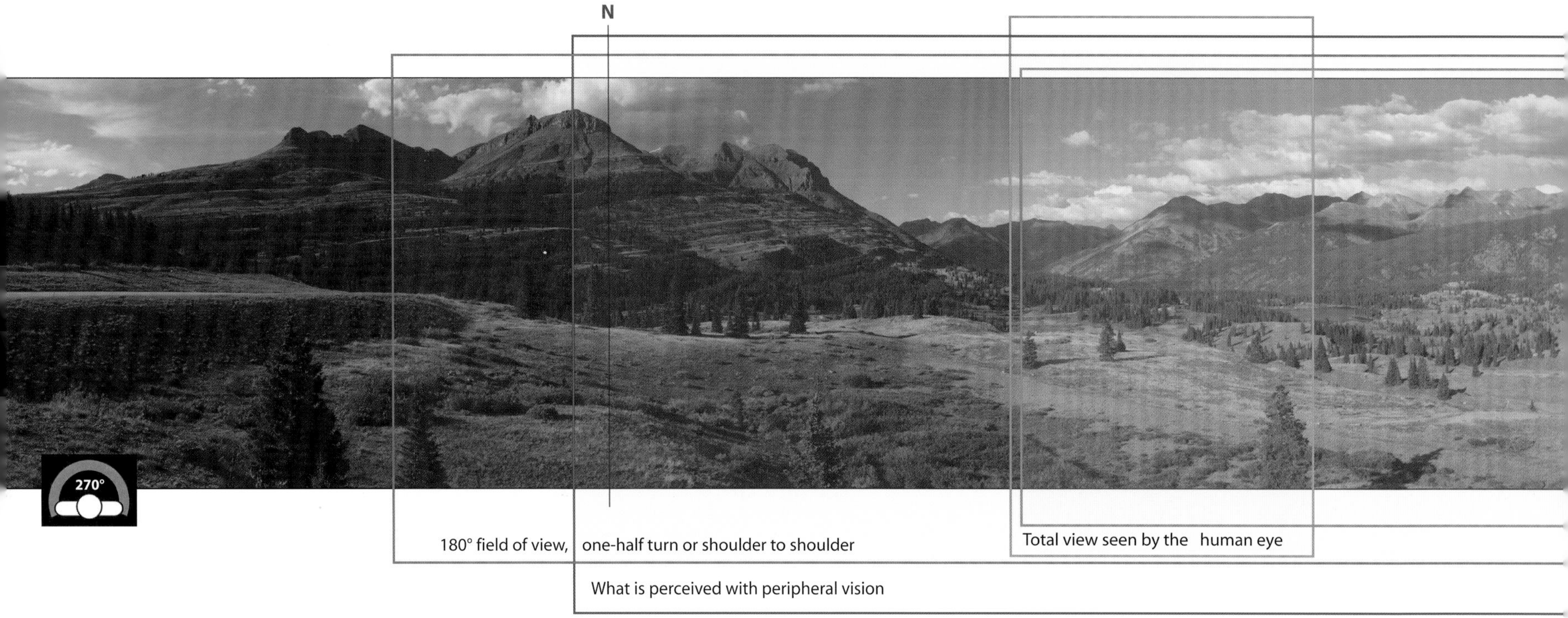
N
270°
180° field of view,
one-half turn or shoulder to shoulder
Total view seen by the human eye
What is perceived with peripheral vision

scene, the sun is behind the camera and at a slight angle, giving the mountains shadows and dimension. Photos taken in early morning and late afternoon often have a wide exposure range from left to right. This is particularly true when the sun is to the extreme right or left of the scene. Part of the scene will have full sunlight on the flanks of the mountains and other parts of the scene will be totally in the shadows. Large, dense clouds may also produce exposure problems because of their shadows.

Artists began creating panoramic images shortly after photography's invention in 1939.

Lens flare can ruin otherwise good photographs, and is especially important to avoid with panoramas. Lens flare is glare on the picture caused by the sun reflecting off the many glass elements of the lens. It may appear as streaks or large pentagon-shaped spots of light on the photo. Sometimes lens flare will add an interesting element to a photo, but with panoramas it can appear multiple times. You can eliminate the possibility of lens flare during an exposure by shading the front of the lens with a hand, hat, or lens hood. Photoshop can also remove lens flare from digital photographs.

Once you've taken all your images, merge them using Adobe Photoshop. The resulting file will likely be a very large document—100mb or more. I work on a Mac laptop with a 17-inch screen. The wide screen makes it easier to work with panoramas. Using a laptop allows me to merge my photos immediately after taking them. This way, I can confirm that all has gone according to plan. Mistakes can be corrected on site.

E
S
90° field of view, one-quarter turn
View captured by a 35mm camera with a 50mm lens

What the Eye Sees

The human eye can focus on about 15 degrees of a scene and can "see" about 50 degrees of the scene. Peripheral vision allows you to perceive about 100 degrees of a scene. You can perceive color and motion with your peripheral vision, but cannot discern much detail.

The panorama photographs in this book cover 90 to 360 degrees of a scene. A photo that is 90 degrees is 1/4 of a full turn. Standing in one location and casually turning your head would produce a view of 90 degrees. A view of 180 degrees is from shoulder to shoulder. A photo of 270 degrees covers a view from behind your left shoulder to an area behind your right shoulder (Molas Pass Panorama above).

Viewing a 360-degree scene would require that you turn completely around. A photo of more than 360 degrees would have something on the far left side of the photo that would also appear on the far right side of the photo.

What the Camera Sees

A 35mm camera uses film that is 35mm wide. The area of a picture on the film is actually 24mm by 36mm. The focal length of the camera lens determines how much of a scene will be captured on the film. A standard lens on a 35mm camera—about 50mm in focal length—sees about 50 degrees of a scene, which is similar to what the eye sees. Longer telephoto lenses see a smaller area, and wide-angle lenses see a larger area.

Further Reading

Arps, Louisa Ward. *High Country Names: Rocky Mountain National Park and Indian Peaks*. Boulder: Johnson Books, 1994.

Baars, Donald L. *A Traveler's Guide to the Geology of the Colorado Plateau*. Salt Lake City: University of Utah Press, 2002.

Becker, Cynthia S. *Chipeta: Queen Of The Ute*. Montrose, Colo.: Western Reflections Publishing Co., 2003.

Bonney, Elwood P. *William Henry Jackson, an Intimate Portrait: The Elwood P. Bonney Journal*. Denver, Colo.: Colorado Historical Society, 2000.

Borneman, Walter R. *Marshall Pass: Denver & Rio Grande Gateway to the Gunnison Country.* Colorado Springs, Colo.: Century One Press, 1980.

Bright, William. *Colorado Place Names*. Boulder, Colo.: Johnson Books, 2004.

Buchholtz, C. W. *Rocky Mountain National Park: A History.* Boulder, Colo.: Colorado Associated University Press, 1983.

Calvert, Patricia. *Zebulon Pike: Lost in the Rockies*. New York: Benchmark Books, 2003.

Carson, Phil. *Across the Northern Frontier: Spanish Explorations in Colorado.* B oulder, Colo.: Johnson Books, 1998.

Cassidy, James G. *Ferdinand V. Hayden: Entrepreneur of Science*. Lincoln, Neb.: University of Nebraska Press, 2000.

Chronic, Halka. *Roadside Geology of Colorado.* Missoula, Mont.: Mountain Press Pub. Co., 2002.

Clamp, Cathy L. *Road to Riches: The Great Railroad Race to Aspen.* Montrose, Colo.: Western Reflections Pub. Co., 2003.

Dawdy, Doris Ostrander. *George Montague Wheeler: The Man and the Myth.* Athens, Ohio: Swallow Press/Ohio University Press, 1993.

Decker, Peter R. *The Utes Must Go!: American Expansion and the Removal of a People*. Golden, Colo.: Fulcrum Pub., 2004.

Engel, Charles M. *The Galloping Goose: Story of the Unique Little Train That Fought to Keep Alive Otto Mears' Narrow Gauge Railroad in the Mountains of Southwest Colorado.* Rico, Colo.: Larry & Marilyn Pleasant, 1979.

Ferrell, Mallory Hope. *The South Park Line.* Mukilteo, Wash.: Hundman Pub., 2003.

Flint, Richard, and Shirley Cushing Flint. *The Coronado Expedition to Tierra Nueva: The 1540–1542 Route Across the Southwest.* Niwot, Colo.: University Press of Colorado, 1997.

Gantt, Paul H. *The Case of Alfred Packer, The Man-Eater*. Denver, Colo.: University Of Denver Press, 1952.

Griswold, P. R. *The Alpine Tunnel Story: A 21st Century Look at a 19th Century Engineering Marvel.* Brighton, CO: Sherm Conners Pub., 2003.

Harrell, Thomas H. *William Henry Jackson: An Annotated Bibliography, 1862 to 1995.* Nevada City, Ca.: Carl Mautz Pub., 1995.

Helmuth, Ed. *The Passes of Colorado: an Encyclopedia of Watershed Divides.* Boulder, Colo.: Pruett, 1994.

Jackson, Clarence S. *Jackson, William Henry, 1843–1942: Picture Maker of the Old West.* New York: Scribner, 1947.

Jackson, William Henry. *William Henry Jackson's "The Pioneer Photographer."* Santa Fe: Museum Of New Mexico Press, 2005.

Jackson, William Henry, and John Fielder. *Colorado: 1870–2000.* Englewood, Colo.: Westcliffe Publishers, 1999.

Jackson, William Henry. *Time Exposure: The Autobiography of William Henry Jackson*. Albuquerque, N.M.: University Of New Mexico Press, 1986.

Jocknick, Sidney. *Early Days on the Western Slope of Colorado and Campfire Chats with Otto Mears, the Pathfinder, from 1870 to 1883.* Glorieta, N.M.: Rio Grande Press, 1969.

Kaplan, Michael. *Otto Mears: Paradoxical Pathfinder*. Silverton, Colo.: San Juan County Book Co., 1982.

Kaufman, Duane E. *The History of Rio Grande Motor Way, Inc.: A Subsidiary of The Denver And Rio Grande Western Railroad Company.* Denver, CO: Kaufman Pub., 1996.

Lawlor, Laurie. *Window on the West: The Frontier Photography of William Henry Jackson*. New York: Holiday House, 1999.

Lemassena, R. A. *Denver and Rio Grande Western Superpower Railroad of the Rockies.* Lynchburg, VA: TLC Pub. Inc., 1999.

Lindberg, James. *Rocky Mountain Rustic: Historic Buildings of the Rocky Mountain National Park Area*. Estes Park, Colo.: Rocky Mountain Nature Association, 2004.

Ludwig, Jim. *Beyond The Glory Hole: A Memoir of a Climax Miner.* Buena Vista, Colo.: Pleasant Avenue Nursery, Inc., 2005.

Magsamen, Kurt. *Cycling Colorado's Mountain Passes.* Golden, Colo.: Fulcrum Pub., 2002.

MacDonald, Dougald. *Longs Peak: The Story of Colorado's Favorite Fourteener.* Englewood, Colo.: Westcliffe Publishers, 2004.

Noel, Thomas J. *Colorado, 1870–2000, Revisited: The History Behind the Images.* Englewood, Colo.: Westcliff Pub., 2001.

Osterwald, Doris B. *Cinders & Smoke: A Mile by Mile Guide for the Durango and Silverton Narrow Gauge Railroad.* Hugo, Colo.: Western Guideways, 2001.

Park County, Office Of Tourism. "Guanella Pass: Scenic And Historic Byway: Tour Guide." Fairplay, Colo.: Park County Tourism Office, 1992.

Pettem, Silvia. *Mountains & Passes: A Guide to the Colorado Rockies.* Frederick, Colo.: Renaissance House, 1987.

Pickering, James H. *America's Switzerland: Estes Park and Rocky Mountain National Park, the Growth Years.* Boulder, Colo.: University Press of Colorado, 2005.

Pickering, James H. *Enos Mills' Colorado.* Boulder, Colo.: Johnson Books, 2006.

Prescott, Jerome. *The Unspoiled West: The Western Landscape as Seen by its Greatest Photographer.* New York: Smithmark, 1994.

Richardson, Robert W. *Robert W. Richardson's Rio Grande: Chasing the Narrow Gauge.* Forest Park, Ill.: Heimburger House Pub., 2002.

Rohrbough, Malcolm J. *Aspen: The History of a Silver-Mining Town, 1879–1893.* Boulder, Colo.: University Press of Colorado, 2000.

Roscoe, Gerald. *Westward: The Epic Crossing of the American Landscape.* New York: Monacelli Press, 1995.

Royem, Robert T. *An American Classic: The Durango & Silverton Narrow Gauge Railroad.* Durango, Colo: Limelight Press, 1995.

Scamehorn, H. Lee. *Mill & Mine: The CF&I in the Twentieth Century.* Lincoln, Neb.: University of Nebraska Press, 1992.

Smith, Duane A. *Durango & Silverton Narrow Gauge: A Quick History.* Ouray, Colo.: Western Reflections, 1998.

Souza, D. M. *John Wesley Powell.* New York: Franklin Watts, 2004.

Stallones, Jared. *Zebulon Pike and the Explorers of the American Southwest.* New York: Chelsea House Publishers, 1992.

Starrs James E. *Alfred G. Packer Victims Exhumation Project, Lake City, Colorado.* Washington, D.C., Scientific Sleuthing, 1989.

Strong, William K. *The Remarkable Railroad Passes of Otto Mears.* Silverton, Colo.: San Juan County Book Co., 1988.

Towler, Sureva. *The History of Skiing at Steamboat Springs.* Steamboat Springs, Colo.: Routt County Research, 1987.

Tucker, E. F. *Otto Mears and the San Juans.* Montrose, Colo.: Western Reflections Pub. Co., 2001.

Turner, Robert D. *The Thunder of Their Passing: A Tribute to the Denver & Rio Grande's Narrow Gauge and the Cumbres & Toltec Scenic Railroad.* Winlaw, B.C.: Sono Nis Press, 2003.

Waitley, Douglas. *William Henry Jackson: Framing the Frontier.* Missoula, Mont.: Mountain Press Pub. Co., 1998.

West, Elliott. *The Contested Plains: Indians, Goldseekers, & the Rush to Colorado.* Lawrence, Kan.: University Press of Kansas, 1998.

Wiatrowski, Claude A. *Railroads of Colorado: Your Guide to Colorado's Historic Trains and Railway Sites.* Stillwater, Minn.: Voyageur Press, 2002.

Williamson, Ruby G. *Otto Mears, Pathfinder of the San Juan: His Family and Friends.* Gunnison, Colo.: B & B Printers, 1981.

Photo Credits

All contemporary photographs were taken by Rick Spitzer. Historic photographs, listed here, were provided courtesy of the Denver Public Library (DPL) and the Colorado Historical Society (CHS). When known, historic photographers are also listed.

Page	Photo	Call number	Photographer or collection
28	Horse & Buggy	DPL 00120161	Lake, Harry H., c.1910
30	Car on Berthoud Pass	DPL 00185511	Rhoads, H.M., 1917
72	Eisenhower Tunnel	DPL 11000108	Gordon, John, 1970
102	Fremont Pass	DPL 00300338	Jackson, W.H., c.1882
103	Fremont Pass	CHS 20100849	Jackson, W.H., c.1882
121	Gold Dredge	DPL 10063038	Fick, William L., 1940
128	Mason Bogie	DPL 00073235	McClure, L.C., c.1886
129	Charcoal Kilns	DPL 10014033	Unknown, c.1890
141	Aspen Boat Tow	DPL 00200737	Southworth, W.A., 1943
145	Quarry Buildings	DPL 0071995	McClure, L.C., c.1913
145	Tomb of the Unknowns	DPL 10012283	Unknown, 1931
174	San Luis Rail Line	DPL 00401076	Richardson, R.W., 1950
178	Train at Snowshed	DPL 00008173	Perry, Otto, 1939
179	Marshall Pass Grade	CHS 20102043	Jackson, W.H., c.1870
180	Marshall Pass Snow Shed	DPL 00310403	Unknown, c.1890
184	Dallas Divide View	CHS 20102019	Jackson, W.H., c.1880
193	Freight Train	DPL 00008118	Perry, Otto, 1945
194	Town of Telluride	CHS 20100695	Jackson, W.H., c.1880
200	Abandoned Mine	DPL 00135209	Beam, George L., c.1920
201	Toll Road	CHS 20103853	Jackson, W.H., c.1884
206	Otto Mears & Train	DPL 11001425	Goodman, Charles D., 1912
210	Burnot Treaty	DPL 10030679	Unknown, 1874
226	Car on Wolf Creek	DPL 00185526	Rhoads, H.M., c1925

Index

Bold-faced numbers refer to the pages describing the individual passes.

INTERNATIONAL STANDARD BOOK NUMBER: 978-1-56579-598-3

COVER AND TEXT DESIGN: Rebecca Finkel

PUBLISHED BY:
Westcliffe Publishers,
a Big Earth Publishing company
1637 Pearl St., Suite 201
Boulder, Colorado 80302

PRINTED in Canada by Friesens

9 8 7 6 5 4 3 2 1

LIBRARY OF CONGRESS CATALOGING-IN-PUBLICATION DATA:
Spitzer, Rick.
Colorado mountain passes : the state's most accessible high country roadways / by Rick Spitzer.
p. cm.
Includes bibliographical references and index.
ISBN 978-1-56579-598-3
1. Mountain passes—Colorado—Guidebooks. 2. Automobile travel—Colorado—Guidebooks. 3. Photography, Panoramic. I. Title.

F782.A16S758 2009
917.8804'34—dc22 2008052050

PLEASE NOTE: Risk is always a factor in backcountry and high-mountain travel. Many of the activities described in this book can be dangerous, especially when weather is adverse or unpredictable, and when unforeseen events or conditions create a hazardous situation. The author has done his best to provide the reader with accurate information about backcountry travel, as well as to point out some of its potential hazards. It is the responsibility of the users of this guide to learn the necessary skills for safe backcountry travel, and to exercise caution in potentially hazardous areas, especially on glaciers and avalanche-prone terrain. The author and publisher disclaim any liability for injury or other damage caused by backcountry traveling or performing any other activity described in this book.

The author and publisher of this book have made every effort to ensure the accuracy and currency of its information. Nevertheless, books can require revisions. Please feel free to let us know if you find information in this book that needs to be updated, and we will be glad to correct it for the next printing. Your comments and suggestions are always welcome.

FOR MORE INFORMATION about other fine books and calendars from Westcliffe Publishers, a Big Earth Publishing company, please contact your local bookstore, call us at 1-800-258-5830, or visit us on the Web at bigearthpublishing.com.

Cover Photo: Red Mountain near Red Mountain Pass